All There Is

ALSO BY DAVE ISAY

*Listening Is an Act of Love: A Celebration of American Life
from the StoryCorps Project*

Mom: A Celebration of Mothers from StoryCorps

All There Is

Love Stories from StoryCorps

DAVE ISAY

THE PENGUIN PRESS

New York

2012

THE PENGUIN PRESS
Published by the Penguin Group
Penguin Group (USA) Inc., 375 Hudson Street, New York, New York 10014,
U.S.A. • Penguin Group (Canada), 90 Eglinton Avenue East, Suite 700,
Toronto, Ontario, Canada M4P 2Y3 (a division of Pearson Penguin Canada Inc.)
Penguin Books Ltd, 80 Strand, London WC2R 0RL, England • Penguin
Ireland, 25 St. Stephen's Green, Dublin 2, Ireland (a division of Penguin Books
Ltd) • Penguin Books Australia Ltd, 250 Camberwell Road, Camberwell,
Victoria 3124, Australia (a division of Pearson Australia Group Pty Ltd) •
Penguin Books India Pvt Ltd, 11 Community Centre, Panchsheel Park,
New Delhi—110 017, India • Penguin Group (NZ), 67 Apollo Drive, Rosedale,
Auckland 0632, New Zealand (a division of Pearson New Zealand Ltd) •
Penguin Books (South Africa) (Pty) Ltd, 24 Sturdee Avenue, Rosebank,
Johannesburg 2196, South Africa

Penguin Books Ltd, Registered Offices:
80 Strand, London WC2R 0RL, England

First published in 2012 by The Penguin Press,
a member of Penguin Group (USA) Inc.

10 9 8 7 6 5 4 3 2 1

Library of Congress Cataloging-in-Publication Data

All there is : love stories from Storycorps / [edited and with an introduction by]
Dave Isay.
p. cm.
ISBN 978-1-59420-321-3
1. Love—Anecdotes.   2. United States—Biography—Anecdotes.
3. Interviews—United States.   4. Oral history.   5. StoryCorps (Project)
I. Isay, David.   II. StoryCorps (Project)
HQ801.A2A55 2012
302.3—dc23
2011029942

Printed in the United States of America
Set in Horley Old Style MT
Designed by Amanda Dewey

IN MEMORY OF
LILLIE MAE LOVE 1957–2010

Love is all there is . . . When you take your last breath you remember the people you love, how much love you inspired, and how much love you gave.

—LILLIE LOVE, *StoryCorps Facilitator*

Lillie Love with fellow Facilitator Anthony Knight
at StoryCorps Atlanta

CONTENTS

Introduction   *1*

Author's Note   *5*

FOUND   *7*

LOST   *57*

FOUND AT LAST   *101*

Acknowledgments   *153*

StoryCorps in Brief   *155*

All There Is

INTRODUCTION

StoryCorps launched in October 2003, when we opened our first booth in Grand Central Terminal in New York City. It's a very simple idea. You make an appointment to bring in anyone you want to honor by listening. When you arrive at the booth you're met by a StoryCorps facilitator who takes you inside and sits you across a small table from, say, your grandmother. You face one another, a microphone in front of each of you, and for the next forty minutes you ask questions and listen. Many people think of their interview sessions as: If I had only forty minutes left with this person, what would I want to ask?

Needless to say, the interviews are often quite intense. I am always hearing from participants who say that the time they spent recording at StoryCorps was among the most important forty minutes of their lives. At the end of the session you walk out with a CD of your interview, and with your permission, a second copy goes to the American Folklife Center at the Library of Congress, so that your great-great-great-grandchildren can someday get to know your grandmother through her voice and story.

Since our launch StoryCorps has spread from coast to coast. To date nearly seventy-five thousand people, representing the breadth of the American experience, have participated in the project. Millions more have heard or seen edited excerpts of these interviews on NPR, PBS, and the Web—or in books like this. We hope that recording a StoryCorps interview reminds participants how much their lives matter and that experiencing these stories illustrates the power, strength, and wisdom we can find in the voices of the people all around us when we take the time to listen.

The book you hold in your hands cuts right to the heart of our efforts. StoryCorps is by its nature a project about the transmission of wisdom across generations. Almost all of the interviews we collect touch on the great themes of human existence, and—as we've learned after recording thousands upon thousands of sessions—there can be no question that the greatest of these themes is love.

While conversations about love in all its forms are captured through StoryCorps, we chose to devote this book to stories about romantic love. *All There Is* is divided into three sections, which correspond to the three types of love stories we hear about most often: falling in love; remembering a loved one; and finding love unexpectedly after assuming it was no longer in the cards.

Over the past eight years I've been astonished and delighted by the stories that spin out of our booths and land on my desk each week. They speak to the enduring and redemptive power of love. They make my spirit soar. In a culture that often feels consumed by all that's phony or famous, these stories give me hope and remind me to try to live life without regrets. I hope they do the same for you.

*A*ll *There Is* is dedicated to Lillie Love, our beloved Atlanta-based facilitator who died unexpectedly in 2010. The wisdom and goodness contained in the pages of this book are a testament to the life she lived. Lillie Mae Love will never be forgotten.

—*Dave Isay, September 2011*

AUTHOR'S NOTE

The following stories were edited from transcripts of StoryCorps interviews that typically run forty minutes. We aimed to distill these interviews without altering the tone or meaning of the original sessions. At times tense and usage were changed, and a word or two were added for clarity. We did not use ellipses to indicate omitted text; in the following pages ellipses indicate speech trailing off or a pause in speech or conversation.

Words and phrases that read well are not always the strongest spoken moments, and the reverse is also the case. As a result, a story may vary slightly from audio to print.

Participants gave permission for their stories to be published in this book, and each story was fact-checked. A few participants requested that their ages not be included, and we honored that request.

Found

GAYLE TERRIS NEWBY, 77,

talks with her husband,

FRANK NEWBY, 79

Gayle Terris Newby: After I graduated from high school, my parents couldn't afford college, so I went to nurse's training school at the general hospital in Indianapolis. One day my patient's son told me that he was really crazy about my friend Betty, who was working on the ward with me, and asked if I could get him a date. I said, "I'll try." Betty said, "Okay, but I'm not going on a single date." So he got two guys, and I got another girl, and we went on a triple date.

On the day of the date I'd spent all afternoon on the roof sunbathing. I was red as a beet, my hair was a mess, and I really didn't want to go. As we were walking down the stairs I saw the three guys sitting there, and I said to my friend, "Look at the hick with no tie; I'll bet I get stuck with him." And I did.

I knew that he didn't have any money. They wanted to stop for a hamburger and a Coke, and he just frankly told me, "I can't afford it." Somehow or other that seemed honest to me.

I said, "Let's just sit in the car and talk." And talk we did. Talked ourselves right into love and marriage.

I called him, and we decided we wanted to see each other again. So he came to the hospital to pick me up. Unfortunately, my mother and father's best friends had come in from Chicago that day, and they wanted to take me out to lunch. Now to me, meeting with people who had come all the way from Chicago to Indianapolis was more important than meeting this boy who I had only met once. So I stood him up.

You were really mad, weren't you?

Frank Newby: I waited longer for you that day than I've ever waited for anybody in my life. I don't think I was mad; I was disgusted. I just wrote you off—no one did that to me— and so I went back to work at the filling station. I worked Monday night, worked Tuesday night, and Wednesday evening the manager came back and said, "Frank, you've got a telephone call." I couldn't think of anyone I had ever told where I was working or who had the telephone number, but it was you on the phone. You started explaining to me what happened, and sucker that I was, I accepted the apology. Since I had the next day off, I suggested that we go to Turkey Run State Park, which is about sixty miles from Indianapolis. That Thursday was one of the most idyllic days of my life.

On Friday I took you out to the farm to meet my mother and father.

Gayle: And I wanted you to meet my mother and father

too. We went on Saturday. That was when my mother said to you, "I hope you're not thinking about marrying my daughter, because you'll marry her over my dead body!" But we got married the next Sunday, and she didn't die.

Frank: I told my dad Saturday afternoon, "If you can find us a minister, we're going to get married tomorrow." He went out and found the same minister that had married him and my mother twenty-three years before. He pulled the minister right out of the revival meeting.

I was an avid gardener, and I had over a thousand gladiolas in full bloom. My mother cut practically all of those glads, and the house was absolutely gorgeous with flowers everywhere you looked. So we were married with your two best friends. I had my brother as my best man, and my grandmother and grandfather. That was the wedding party.

I had twenty dollars in my pocket. I had borrowed forty dollars from Dad for the honeymoon, but in the rush and the excitement of the wedding, I forgot to get it. We got halfway to Lake Shafer on the honeymoon when I discovered that I only had the twenty.

Gayle: So we honeymooned on twenty dollars.

Frank: We found a motel for three dollars a night. We discovered a beer garden overlooking Lake Shafer. We'd get a hamburger and a bottle of beer for, I think, seventy-five cents. So we lived three days and three nights on twenty dollars.

Gayle: On hamburgers, beer, and love. We've had fifty-seven great years of marriage, and I've never once regretted a three-day courtship.

Recorded in Las Cruces, New Mexico, on September 2, 2007.

MICHAEL FAZIO, 50,

talks with his wife,

SONYA BAKER, 40

Michael Fazio: I worked for the New York State Thruway Authority as a toll collector for about seventeen years.

Sonya Baker: At the time I was living in Woodstock, New York, and I would drive the Thruway pretty regularly to go to New York City for auditions and lessons and that kind of thing. I saw you one day, and you were very friendly and desperately cute. I remember one night when it was really foggy, I said, "I don't know how you deal with this." You said, "Well, it's a job."

I didn't see you for six months, and then I came through one day and you were counting money. I said, "How you doing?" And you're, like, "How you doing." And then you looked up and said, "Where you been?!" And I said, "I've been here. Where've you been?!" You said, "Well, you must've been coming through the wrong lane!" I said, "Who's to know what the right lane is, buddy?" And you said, "Well, I'll put a cone in my lane. It'll be like keeping a candle in the window for you."

I started making excuses to take the Thruway and started looking for the orange pylons—I almost wrecked on several occasions trying to cross lanes. So I would come through your lane regularly, and we started talking.

Michael: How did you feel about talking to some strange guy in a tollbooth?

Sonya: To be honest, I hadn't had a real date for two years, and I just thought, *This is a step in the right direction.*

After about three or four months, I went through and I said, "Hey, what do I get if you forget to put the cone up?" And you said, "You name it." I said, "Will you take me to dinner?" And you said, "Well, I got to remember not to put the cone up then." And I said, "Just call me," and gave you my phone number. I drove through and thought I was a total ding-a-ling for giving the toll guy my phone number! Of course, my friends thought I was a lunatic, and that if I was going to meet you it better well be in a public place—because what do I know about you? But any friend that has seen us together has never wondered why we're together. They always say, Of course: Sonya and Mike. I mean, what they have together is obvious.

I never, never thought I'd get married. So I always say, Since I never thought I was getting married, I certainly was only going to do it once. So if you hate me, that's too bad. Tough it

out! Because I'm it for you and you're
it for me!

Michael: I don't hate you, Sonya
Baker. I love you.

Sonya: The great part is, it's never
felt like there was a time that we had to
tough it out. There have certainly been
challenges that you and I have risen to
together, but there's nobody I'd rather
travel through life with than you.

*Recorded in Murray, Kentucky,
on October 2, 2005.*

JOEY LEON GUERRERO, 35,

talks with his wife,

DELORA DENISE LEON GUERRERO, 28

Joey Leon Guerrero: The first time we met, I stepped into your office and I asked you to sign one of my papers—I guess it was for my meal card. But we didn't talk at all until we got deployed and I heard that you were coming to Company B.

Delora Denise Leon Guerrero: You sent me a couple of e-mails, but I was there to work. I was focused, driven. I was, like, *We're in Iraq. There's no time for romance or relationships.*

So we spent four months as friends, getting to know one another, seeing each other at work.

During that friendship phase I heard you talking about your family, and I loved it. I'm very family oriented too. I also noticed your leadership—the way you talked to your soldiers and your supervisors, how you carried yourself, the way you dressed, how your weapon was always clean. You didn't let anything slip by. I liked how driven you were. And as we became friends, I liked how you were opening up to me—you were so honest and real.

Joey: But you gave me the cold shoulder. So I was, like, *I'll stay focused on being friends for now.* Because I knew one day you were going to change your mind.

Delora: And then the defining moment was when I was about to leave on R&R, but a sandstorm kept me in Baghdad. We were outside, and you were helping me with my bags by the door of the tent. All of a sudden we get indirect fire— mortars started falling. *Boom! Boom! Boom!* It wasn't the first time I had heard mortars, but it was the first time I was standing outside talking while they were going off.

So I ran to the bunker. Eventually, you came in kind of casually, because you were seasoned. And then we were crouching across from each other in the bunker, waiting for the all clear. I was just looking at you, and it was like a romantic movie scene where all the visions of the last four months come into play: everything we talked about; how you talked to your kids on the phone; the fact that you called your mother; how you treated me. All of it came together while I was looking at you, and I thought, *You know what? Life is way too short to pass you up.* And I think it was that moment where it changed from friendship to, *I can't let this one go or I'm a fool.*

When I went on R&R, I had you on my mind. And when I got back we would walk every night just to get away from the other soldiers and talk. Our romantic moments were walking to the bunkers. Doesn't really sound romantic, I guess: being fully dressed in uniform with a weapon slung on your back . . .

Joey: . . . But from our perspective, we did what normal couples would do. We just did it as a couple in Iraq.

Delora: You picked out a ring online. And when you handed me the box, more mortars hit. We had to evacuate and go back into the bunkers. I thought, *Is this a sign?*

Later that day, you walked me home.

Joey: That's when I got down on my knees with my weapon slung on my back, hoping we weren't going to get hit. And it wasn't your traditional engagement ring box—it was more like a post office box—and I tore that open and said, "Would you marry me?"

Delora: I was kind of hesitant at first—being proposed to in Iraq is not what every girl dreams of. But I knew you were the one for me. So when you said, "Do you want to wait?" I said, "No. This is where we are. This is the moment."

Joey: You didn't turn your back on me. You gave me  a chance, and you accepted me. I can't ask for anything better than you.

Recorded in Frederick, Maryland, on May 22, 2010.

BOBBI CÔTÉ-WHITACRE, 58,

talks with her wife,

SANDI CÔTÉ-WHITACRE, 59

Bobbi Côté-Whitacre: Do you remember what it was like when we were nineteen and in love—and couldn't tell anyone?

Sandi Côté-Whitacre: I remember feeling: *I have found the person I'm going to spend the rest of my life with.* Everything that I believed in—the core things that I felt were important in life—you did also.

Bobbi: We met in the middle of a war, and we fell in love to Bob Hope singing, "Thanks for the Memory." After a few months of dating we decided that we would get a three-day pass and go to Atlanta and get "married." This was 1968. We went to this cheesy little motel in Atlanta and got a Gideon's Bible. I remember reading the story of Ruth to you, and you reading it to me, and us committing ourselves to each other. And you know? That was almost forty years ago, but I still feel the same way today.

Then we moved to Ohio.

Sandi: [*Laughs.*] Your hometown, Bowling Green. The second day that we were there your mother came by and told me that it was a small town, that your father was a prominent doctor, that everybody knew everybody, and that she would give us three days to get out of town so that we wouldn't disgrace your father, his practice, or your extended family.

Bobbi: We didn't leave. And so they sent me to a psychiatrist to see if they could "fix" me. That obviously didn't work. [*Laughs.*]

Sandi: But then—years later—your mom all of a sudden decided that her daughter should have the right to marry.

Bobbi: My mom had been diagnosed with a brain hemorrhage, and she wanted to walk us down the aisle before she died. And this is the same woman that gave us three days to get out of town!

Sandi: We were living in Vermont, and when they voted for civil union in 2000, we said, "Okay, we'll have a civil union." We had it in your mom's backyard. It was a beautiful ceremony, and I remember the minister saying, "Bobbi and Sandi did it backward: They did all of the committing stuff, and then got married."

For the first time, we got to stand up in front of our friends and family and tell them that we loved each other and that we were going to take care of each other for the rest of our lives. I didn't believe that there was another level that we could reach, but just having the ceremony, and having our friends and family there happy for us, was sort of like being nineteen again and celebrating our love.

Bobbi: But I still wasn't totally happy with something less than marriage. That's the way I was brought up, you know? You find the person you want to spend the rest of your life with and you get married. That's just what you do. Then Massachusetts passed a law allowing gay and lesbian couples to get married, and so we went to Provincetown, Massachusetts.

Sandi: I remember the town clerk telling us that if we could get a judge to waive the three-day waiting period we could get married the next day.

When we got to the court the judge said, "What can I do for you ladies?" And I said, "We want to get married, but we don't want to wait the three days." He said, "That isn't a long time." I said, "After we've waited thirty-four years, it is a very long time!" [*Laughs.*] He said, "Well, I would be happy to sign the waiver. I don't believe the state of Massachusetts should make you wait one day longer."

And the next morning we had a justice of the peace say the words out in her yard. She had a nice lilac tree, and she declared us to be married in the state of Massachusetts.

Bobbi: We went out and we bought T-shirts that said JUST MARRIED! We walked on the sand barefoot. At the motel where we were staying, they gave us this beautiful bouquet of flowers.

BOBBI COTE-WHITACRE *(left)*
AND SANDI COTE-WHITACRE

Sandi: It was everything that we had thought it would be.

Bobbi: And now I can call you my wife.

Sandi: And I can call you mine.

Recorded in Burlington, Vermont, on August 18, 2006.

FRANK CARRILLO, 54,

talks with his wife,

NANCY NGAI CARRILLO, 52

Frank Carrillo: I told my mom that my girlfriend was Chinese, and she wasn't happy about it.

Nancy Ngai Carrillo: It was a little nerve-racking meeting her for the first time.

Frank: We were standing in the yard talking to my sister. My mom started banging on pots and pans to make dinner. Her upbringing said that she had to feed this woman that came home with her son, so she opened up the window and she goes, "Hey! Are you guys going to stay around and eat or what?" I asked you, "You want to stay for dinner?" You weren't too sure.

Nancy: I was scared to death of her!

Frank: Hey, don't feel bad. I was scared to death of her too! But I said, "Well, Mom's already making dinner." So you stayed, and to make a long story short, you and my mom became very, very good friends. My mom now has more faith in you than she does in me. I tell her one thing, and she may not believe me, but you tell her the same thing, and she believes it.

Nancy: I think she finally realized that I wasn't going anywhere, and slowly the prejudice eroded.

When my family emigrated here in 1968, the one thing Grandfather told my dad was to be sure the kids didn't marry outside the Chinese race. When we first met and started dating, I was really afraid to introduce you to my parents. I just introduced you as a "friend" for a long time.

Frank: I was known as "Mexican boy," then "Nancy's friend," and then finally I became known as "Frank."

The only person that accepted me right off the bat was your grandmother. Grandma used to stand there and talk to me in Chinese. I had no clue what she was telling me, but I would sit there and listen. I would hold the door open for her; I would help her out of her chair; I would look to see what she needed. And I guess she understood that the same basic values transcended both cultures. She was the one that was actually advocating for us with your parents.

We dated for ten years. When we decided to get married, I sat down with you and said, "I've never waited for anything this long in my life." Your dad didn't want to participate in the marriage. But he finally accepted me after I explained to him, "You know, Dad, we need to get along. If we don't, the only person who's going to suffer is your daughter." After that I became Bob's son-in-law. And that May I was a married man.

One of the biggest problems I see in this world is fear of

the unknown. And I think that raising a child who is Mexican, Puerto Rican, and Chinese is making this world a little bit better, giving people an understanding that we're all the same. I think that relationships like ours are what make this country what it is.

Recorded in Yuma, Arizona, on January 29, 2010.

BILL BLOOM, 90,

talks with his wife,

JANE BLOOM, 84

Bill Bloom: We met in Stillwater, Oklahoma. I think it was the second night I was in town.

Jane Bloom: The women would bake cookies for the service people and the girls would come down to dance, but I was a terrible dancer.

Bill: I remember meeting you there at the USO and asking you to dance, and you said you didn't know how. And I said, "Oh, everybody knows how to dance!" And so I took you out and pushed you around the floor. You learned enough to get by.

Jane: Somewhere along the line you decided that you were going to marry me. I certainly hadn't decided I would marry you. You were an antique. You were twenty-six.

Bill: I think you were nineteen. It was around Christmas vacation, and you'd gone off for a week. When you came back the first thing I said to you was, "Well, I've got some news for you: You and I are going to get married."

You didn't say no. You said, "Oh, I don't think it's possible." And I said, "Why not?" You said, "Well, you're Protestant and I'm Catholic," and I said, "Oh, things like that don't make any difference. We'll work that out." And we did. We got married in Paris.

Jane: Paris, Texas. That was an army camp then. We were married by the priest who was there at the time, in the chapel that's long since been torn down—but the marriage lasted.

During the war I lived with your parents. They seemed to have a little more than my parents in substance and food and heat and house. I was already pregnant with our first child when you went overseas. In those days you were real lucky if you could get a telegram, but if you were out in the field, you couldn't even get that.

Bill: I told you to have it published in *Stars and Stripes.* That's where I found out about David being born.

Jane: When you came back you started right away working with your dad. And you did that for many, many years while we had many, many children—we had eight in nine years, all single births. Eventually we had ten, but we finally managed to put a little time between them. In the meantime we bought a farm with an old farmhouse on it. It was really hard. Chop the wood; keep the house heated. We never made enough money to make our ends meet.

Bill: I think we reached a point where we realized that there were easier ways to earn money.

Jane: Yeah, and you said, "Hey, you can get a job too!"

And I said, "All I know how to do is take care of kids and handle eggs. I think I'll go back to school." Those were different times, you know. Your sister said, "Why in the world are you going to school when you've got a husband?"

I went into the university and told them I was ready to come back to school. The man sort of looked at me funny, and I said, "My children are all grown, I don't have any on the lap or breast or anything else, so I have a lot of free time to go to school." They were really shocked.

So the man said to me, "Well, what are you going to do?" And I said, "You know, I haven't really thought about it, but I think I'll just go on and be a doctor." Here I was, forty years old, looking like anything but a doctor—not even predoctorish—and you were off struggling to pay off the debts and raise the kids. But you stood behind me every drop of the way.

And I did it. I became a doctor. In 1974 I graduated from medical school. All the time you were working to pay off the debts, never complaining at all, just struggling along.

We've been married sixty-four years. We've come through some hard times, but we've had lots of rewards—*lots.*

Recorded in Ann Arbor, Michigan, on September 5, 2008.

TOMÁŠ KUBRIČAN, 32,

interviews his wife,

CAROL MITTLESTEADT, 31

Tomáš Kubričan: I was a student in medical school in Slovakia on a visit at the United States to learn about America. I worked at Paul Bunyan restaurant, and you picked the same place for your summer job.

Carol Mittlesteadt: I saw you on my interview. I walked through the kitchen to meet with the owners, and I saw you standing there. You were this kind of skinny guy with a big apron around his waist, and you were sorting silverware in the kitchen.

Tomáš: I got immediately interested in you. But because of the cultural difference your perception was a little different.

Carol: I got the job, and as I was going about my business through the kitchen, you just kept staring at me. You wouldn't stop looking at me! You were this scrawny guy with great big blue eyes looking at me all the time and never saying anything.

Tomáš: As I learned many years later, you thought that I had some mental disorder. [*Laughs.*]

Carol: I thought you were maybe a little slow, and I kind of felt sorry for you. So I just kind of smiled at you once in a while.

It was your job to make the pancakes every morning. One day you made me these pancakes in the shape of hearts. I knew something was up, and I tried to talk to you, but you didn't really talk back. I didn't know that you didn't speak English.

Tomáš: I was speaking English. Just my English wasn't as good as it should be.

Carol: But obviously, we did find some way to communicate, and we both realized that we kind of liked each other.

Our first date that summer was in Madison. The Wisconsin Chamber Orchestra was playing on the Capitol lawn— it was a nice picnic affair. I came to pick you up, and you were not so appropriately dressed. You were wearing big, saggy jeans and a plastic belt that was almost broken through. But your T-shirt was the best part. It was a big picture of a stein of beer in the shape of a woman's figure and it said TEN REASONS WHY BEER IS BETTER THAN A WOMAN. And this was our first date!

I took you anyway, and we were having a nice picnic and listening to the chamber orchestra. At one point the mood turned really romantic, and you turned to me and you said . . .

Tomáš: "I'm sick of you."

Carol: And I said, "What?"

Tomáš: Well, at the moment I knew I said something

wrong. Translated from Slovak language, that's how we say "I'm lovesick." But reading your facial expression I realized that it probably doesn't mean the same thing in English.

Carol: I decided to give you a second chance anyway.

Tomáš: This first date was July 31, 1996. Then I returned back to Slovakia.

Carol: When I came to Slovakia in January, it was my first trip abroad, and I was very nervous, because we hadn't seen each other since the previous summer. I thought, *What am I doing? I'm crazy! I'm flying halfway across the world to see this guy I haven't seen for months!* But after that, we realized that we had something going on. You were still in medical school in Slovakia, and I needed to return to school in Chicago. So we'd be together for a week or two weeks, and then we'd have to say good-bye.

Tomáš: It usually meant another six months.

Carol: Saying good-bye was always the hardest. But I remember one day we were crossing the street and you turned to me and said in your accent, "Maybe ve could get married."

Tomáš: It's not the most romantic way to propose. But I just said what I felt, and I never regret that. Then I had to call my future father-in-law and with my broken English ask him for your hand. It was really difficult for him to understand what I was saying on the phone. I just remember I was sweating a lot.

So we got what I needed to enter States, and we got married

in 1999. Our wedding date was July 31, 1999—exactly three years later after our first date. But I dressed up better for the wedding.

Carol: After our wedding we lived in Madison for a while, and you finished medical school, and finally your dream to become a doctor has come true. It's been a hard road.

Tomáš: This whole process probably would be much more different if you didn't help me. So hopefully in near future, I'll be able to pay back.

Carol: You already have. When things get difficult, I think about what you have given up—your family, your medical career in Slovakia, your language, your culture, *everything* to come and be with me. And that nothing can be too horrible with you by my side.

Recorded in Milwaukee, Wisconsin, on February 3, 2007.

HUNNY REIKEN, 80,

talks with her husband,

ELLIOT REIKEN, 86

Hunny Reiken: I have a twin sister, Bunny. And you have a twin brother, Danny. When we met we were sixteen and a half, and we were waitresses in a hotel. You and Danny were musicians in a band. And we thought you were handsome, which you still are.

Elliot Reiken: At first, you and your sister couldn't tell us apart and we couldn't tell you two apart. Remember how you decided on which one you were going with?

Hunny: We said, "With whomever we walk." So I asked, "What's your name?" And you told me, "Elliot." And for the next few days I'd always ask, "Elliot?" Within a few weeks, I knew Elliot. I never went over to Danny thinking it was you. And lo and behold, those were the ones we ended up with. I walked with you; I married you. Bunny walked with Danny; she married Danny. Lucky us, because I don't think it would've worked the other way.

You were tall. You were handsome. And to me, being a

musician made you glamorous and sexy, automatically. You took me out for my seventeenth birthday. We saw *Oklahoma!* on Broadway. I had never dated anyone else, but from then on I knew I loved you, and there was no chance of separating us.

Elliot: We didn't skip a beat. Right from the summer romance into the winter, and on and on.

Hunny: We were married at Temple Beth El in Borough Park, Brooklyn. You and I were married the same day as Bunny and Danny—that was quite a big affair. We had a double wedding. And it was two brides, two grooms, one set of parents for each.

Bunny and I had identical gowns. The flowers were identical.

Elliot: We both went on our honeymoon by train to Miami Beach. But we went on different trains and to different hotels, so that people wouldn't stare at us.

What did you think about marrying me so many years ago? Did you think it would turn out this many years?

Hunny: I never thought anybody lasts this many years! To me divorce was not a foreign word, because if you remember, Elliot, my mother was a divorced woman when she was in her thirties. But I was sure you were the right one. And you know what? I was right. You *are* the right one for me.

I like the way you kiss. You bowled me over sixty-some-odd years ago with your way of kissing, and the way you hold me when we dance. You're not a fantastic dancer, but you hold me fantastically, and I feel it. It's genuine.

Elliot: You've told me that many times, but it still makes me feel great.

Hunny: There are times we can be so annoyed at each other, Elliot, and we yell at each other. But when push comes to shove, we let it go, and we're back to our normal selves, because being unhappy is part of being happy.

When two people get married, they say two people become one. No, I don't agree. Two people should remain two people but walk side by side. I've not become Elliot. Elliot has not become Hunny. We remain Hunny and Elliot. And to me, that's important.

Elliot: You made my life complete. And I hope we'll go on for another fifty years.

Hunny: I'll take five good ones. Five good ones, and I'll say, "Thank you, God!"

Recorded in Brooklyn, New York, on May 15, 2010.

SCOTT WALL, 50,

talks with his wife,

ISABEL SOBOZINSKY-WALL, 52

Scott Wall: I was single and feeling lonely on New Year's Eve. I was living in the Bronx at the time, and a few friends asked me to come over to their apartment for champagne, but I was restless, so I wandered the streets of Manhattan. I ended up in the Paris Café, and I happened to look over at the corner of the bar, and there was this ravishingly beautiful woman sitting by herself, wearing a beautiful dress with Ava Gardner gloves and her hair was all done up. So I approached her and introduced myself.

Isabel Sobozinsky-Wall: It was just a little bit after midnight—January 1, 1992, and I thought right away, *Here's somebody special.*

Scott: I was very surprised when you asked me for my ID.

Isabel: I had been told that Manhattan is so big and scary and you just don't know who you're running into. I was from San Francisco, visiting a friend in New York, so I wanted to make sure you were who you said you were. Then you and I just wandered around the Lower East Side.

Scott: We talked all night. When you went back to California, I dropped you off at the airport. I remember we stayed in the parking lot for a couple hours, like we were at some drive-in.

We kept in touch by writing letters, and then we started making cassette tapes. I commuted into Manhattan, and I had a little Walkman, so on those one-hour commutes into town I would just interview anybody I saw. I would interview the brakeman on the subway. I'd say, "I know this girl in San Francisco I really dig, and I'd like you to say hello to her." So I was just sharing my joy about the feelings that I had for you with the world.

Isabel: You even took it to the dentist once!

Scott: I sent them to you as a surprise, and then you started sending them back to me.

Isabel: You asked strangers, but I asked people I knew, like my mom. Also, I worked at the general hospital at the time, and so I'd get to work early and I'd record the coffee grinder.

Scott: I'd get really excited when the mail came in. I kept them in my Walkman, and I played them over and over. We were courting each other from such a long distance, so playing them was comforting. You're only hearing voices, so I was imagining the Golden Gate Bridge in the background. I was just thinking of all these beautiful scenes and trying to imagine what it would be like to be there.

Isabel: We'd also send each other things we wanted to share, small gifts. I knew that you were smitten when you sent me your grandmother's toaster, and there was a card with it that said, "I hope some day to be there with you when you toast my English muffins for me." [*Laughs.*] I used to reread your letters a lot, and of course I used the toaster. And then you sent me the salt and pepper shakers from your grandma too.

Scott: I was giving you all my private possessions.

Isabel: You were gradually moving in without me knowing it. You came out to visit me in April.

Scott: On the plane back, I just said, *This is it. This is the girl.* But I didn't know, how do we make this work?

Over the phone I said I'd like to come out there for an extended stay, and see how it works. You were cautious but encouraging, and so I ended up selling everything I owned and driving out in Daisy, my 1966 Oldsmobile, to stay with you.

Isabel: It took you almost a month. I remember you called, and you said, "I'm across the Golden Gate." So I rushed home, and I opened the window—and there you were!

Scott: It was really just the most incredible experience, coming all that way and knowing that I was going to see this beautiful girl that I had fallen in love with. It was really the pot of gold at the end of the rainbow. So we moved in together. I'm glad we didn't hesitate.

Isabel: In six months we became friends through our letters and our tapes and our phone calls. But the wedding part was later.

Scott: That was seven years in the making. I remember I went to a party one night, and our friend Andrea said to me, "Girlfriends don't want to be girlfriends forever, you know." That's when the lightbulb went off: "Oh, I should ask her to marry me?" And she just nodded. Happiness is happiness. I didn't want anything to change, and really nothing has.

You've made me the happiest man that I know, and I want to thank you for being my friend and my wife and my counselor, my adviser, and my organizer.  And I just want you to know I need you every day.

Isabel: Ditto for me—to all that.

Recorded in San Francisco, California, on February 13, 2011.

PAUL CHOU, 49,

talks with his wife,

KAREN HUANG, 51

Paul Chou: I came out to San Francisco for my family reunion in August of 1990. My cousin Hedy and her then fiancé Jack promised me that they would call some friends who might be willing to go out on a date with me. They went to work, calling these various women. Fortunately, you called them back.

Karen Huang: You were sitting at the restaurant with your cousins, and I thought, *He's pretty good-looking.* [*Laughs.*] We started talking. You were one of the happiest people I have ever come across. And when you would talk about things that you had been doing and things that you wanted to do, it sounded incredibly appealing, like it would just be a fun life with you.

Paul: By the end of the evening I remember you handing me your business card, and I said that I would keep in touch. I called from my family reunion and asked if you would allow me to take you to dinner, and then would you take me to the airport? I guess we continued our conversation on the pay phone rather enthusiastically—I remember my cousins wondering why I was paying no attention to them or the rest of my family, standing on the street for two hours.

We had a great dinner, and then you took me to the airport. You saw me off—no peck on the cheek, nothing like that. But I remember getting on the airplane thinking, *This could be interesting.* So I wrote a letter through the night, and then sent the letter when I got home. And come to find out that you had also done the same thing.

Karen: I was really resisting having any feelings of liking you, because you lived in Pennsylvania, which was extremely far away. I had never been there. And I had this nice career going. I owned a house in San Francisco. I had a whole life in California, so why even get into any kind of entanglement with you? It just seemed crazy. But then, obviously, I really liked you.

We wrote a lot. I think we built up a lot of intimacy with all that communicating. It's like writing an essay every single day about some new topic. We would write about everything.

Paul: A lot happened in those letters, as I remember. I couldn't help being somewhat flirtatious, just because it was kind of fun and innocent enough.

Karen: You were plenty flirtatious, but you didn't make a pass at me for a long time.

Paul: Soon we were spending three hundred dollars a month on phone bills, flying back and forth, so I think we cut to the chase about things.

But for me, the catalyst was when my mom died in a car accident suddenly, in November. I remember I was supposed to meet your family for Thanksgiving.

Karen: You called me, and you said, "I can't come out for my visit, because my mom and dad were in a car crash and my mom passed away." Initially, you didn't want me to come with you.

Paul: It forced me to figure out whether or not you should be a part of this kind of . . . sadness. You hadn't met my mom, hadn't met my dad or my sister. You were still a new relationship for me. That was . . . that was a hard time. And I think, if I regret anything, it's that she never had a chance to meet you. But you really wanted to be a part of my family's life—for good or for bad.

I didn't know if my dad would be willing to meet you for the first time under such duress. Fortunately, he did want to see you. He knew how important you were to me; my mom had put your photo on the refrigerator, which she never did with any of the girlfriends I had before. I will always admire my father for making a sign to welcome you, even though he had a broken arm from the car accident.

Karen: I remember your dad being so warm. Here's somebody who had just lost his wife, and he was very, very sad, but he was still so engaged. I just remember him making me feel very welcome and comfortable.

Paul: It was a tough time, but it built strength between us. As much as I miss my mom, maybe that's what she did for us.

In February, I flew out to Stanford and surprised you.

Karen: I was at work, and my colleague said, "Oh, we forgot to tell you: We have to go across campus to see the new dean at the chapel." So we were kind of jogging across campus, because we were late, and as we walked into the sanctuary I noticed some violin music. It wasn't until we were pretty far into the church that I realized that it was you, and that you were playing the Winter Movement from Vivaldi's *Four Seasons*. I remember you were wearing your tweed jacket, and you were playing all by yourself. There was this older couple sitting in one of the front pews, just in rapt attention, listening to you. I didn't know what was going on: *Why are you doing this performance in the church?* And then I kind of got an inkling. When you finished you came over to me and you asked me if I would marry you. It was incredibly romantic and incredibly surprising.

I remember one of the things I said to you during our vows at the wedding was that I looked forward to seeing your happy face every morning. I still do.

Paul: You know, you are still all I imagined you would be—except more of it. You're smart. You're generous. I guess, most of all, you're just lots of fun to be around. Thanks, Karen. For a wonderful life.

Recorded in Chevy Chase, Maryland, on May 20, 2010.

RACHEL PEREZ SALAZAR, 43,

talks with her husband,

RUBEN PAUL SALAZAR, 39

Rachel Perez Salazar: It was January 10, 2007, and you were working at a computer lab in Waco.

Ruben Paul Salazar: I got to work, and first thing I did was crank up my e-mail. I discovered one that I didn't know who it was from, addressed to "RP Salazar." I figured, *Hey, my e-mail is almost the same exact thing, so they probably sent it to the wrong person.* And so I dug up this Rachel Salazar name, and I wrote a little message—"Hi, Rachel, *holá*, it seems as if this message came to me instead of you. I'm in Waco, Texas, USA." And the salutation was, "Ruben P. Salazar, Chicano Cyclist, Commuter and Community Artist." "PS, how's the weather there in Bangkok?" Because I saw that you were in Bangkok, Thailand.

Rachel: And I wrote to you: "Hi, Ruben, *holá*, thanks for forwarding the message. You'll probably get a few more stray ones now that you've been included in the loop. Weather in Bangkok is lovely; it's the best time to visit. Gracias, Rachel."

Ruben: And so began a chain of your replies to my reply and me replying to your replies, and so on. I just imagined, *Here's this middle-aged woman that's just kind of bored at work—that's why she's replying to me.* But I happened to hover my pointer over your name on one of those e-mails, and a picture of you popped up, and I was, like, *Wow, she's really beautiful! How can I make this picture bigger?* [*Laughs.*] That just blew me away.

Rachel: Every conversation that we had right from the get-go was natural. There was nothing awkward, nothing strange.

Ruben: I kind of just opened myself up and told you who I am, the good things, the bad things. I know I told you repeatedly that I'm a stubborn type of person. I don't think I left anything unsaid. I was excited that this person is halfway around the world, you know? She can't see me, she can't hear me, but I can tell her all these things. It's kind of like sending a letter in a bottle to the ocean.

By February or March, we were on the computer sometimes for four or five hours.

Rachel: I wrote a handwritten letter to you on a plane. I actually managed to write eight pages, and I have it here in front of me. I started describing the flight to you—I wrote to you about the meal, how the flight attendants kept looking at me and wondering, *Who is this girl writing to? She's been writing the whole time.*

I think around page six or seven I got serious and started talking to you about my future: "The future still looks a little bit fuzzy to me. I know life has a way of interrupting the best laid plans, but I am prepared for it." When I look at that statement, in hindsight, *you* are that interruption.

Honestly, I don't think I was thinking about you in any romantic sense, probably until June.

Ruben: Whereas I looked upon you romantically the first time I saw your picture.

Rachel: But then I realized I kept telling you things I didn't even tell my mom. Then you sent me flowers. I kept the card for it; you wrote, "*Chica naranja,* thank you for all you do, and thank you always for this newfound friendship we have happened upon. RPS."

Ruben: It sounds cheesy.

Rachel: I know, but it was romantic. I loved it.

Ruben: I had asked you for your telephone number, because I wanted to hear your voice. At some point I called you, then I finally had a voice to go with the words that I was reading.

Rachel: I was also excited: *Wow! He sounds so real!* By then we were practically best friends.

Ruben: I would talk to my coworkers: "We know so much about each other. In a weird kind of way, I have feelings for her already, but I don't know if she has them back for me." It really felt like you were my girlfriend, even if it was just an electronic thing.

Then you just kind of threw out that you might come to the U.S., because you have family here, and my reply was, "If you're ever in Texas, come over and I'll be glad to show you around the state." I never would have thought in my wildest dreams that you would actually take me up on that!

Rachel: That was August already. We were talking to each other on the phone practically every day, and I was writing to you more. We were past the stage of just talking about the weather. We were easing into talking about more serious things.

I didn't want to show you my feelings. I knew that I was falling in love, but at the back of my mind, there's still that tiny little bit of doubt that this might not work: We were nine thousand miles away from each other—halfway across the world. But at some point I finalized my plans to visit the U.S., and I decided that I was going to go to Texas and meet this guy. But I didn't tell anyone. Everyone would have said, You're foolish to go halfway across the world to meet some strange guy! But I knew in my heart, *I'm meeting my destiny.*

Ruben: And on my end, every relative, every friend, every coworker—*everyone* knew. They're like, "No way she's coming! She doesn't even know you!" You stayed with me for a week.

Rachel: We were e-mailing for eight months, and finally for eight days we were together. I had the greatest time of my life.

Ruben: I remember we were dancing one night, and you mentioned something to the effect that no one . . .

Rachel: —I said you were the sweetest guy I've ever met. No one has ever been that tender to me.

Ruben: I knew right at that moment: I need to say something or do something so that I don't lose you. And so I got on my knee and asked you to marry me.

Rachel: And I said yes. Deep in my heart I knew it was coming, and it was the right thing, and it was the *best* thing.

Two days later I had to go to California and leave you, but I came back, and we got married here in Waco, November 24, 2007.

Ruben: And we just celebrated our third wedding anniversary.

You know what the weird thing is, though? When you told your family that I proposed to you, they weren't so excited. And I would hear that too. When I told people I proposed to Rachel—You what?! Followed by five minutes of laughter. [*Laughs.*] People didn't believe me, and some of them had second thoughts for me. But it was hard to describe to people—you weren't a stranger.

Rachel: Yes, but now they all tell us: You're perfect for

each other. You found the right match!

Ruben: Expect the unexpected. You laid your heart on the line in those e-mails, and you are the way you wrote yourself to be.

Recorded in Waco, Texas, on November 27, 2010.

KELLY KRIEG-SIGMAN, 51,
talks with her husband,
MICHAEL SIGMAN, 55

Kelly Krieg-Sigman: When I first saw you I thought you were an alcoholic. I was involved in community theater, and after rehearsal I would go to a bar in Manitowoc called The Sting. Every time I was there I saw you sitting at the end of the bar all by yourself, hunched over a cup of coffee. And every night at exactly seven minutes to eleven you threw money on the bar, grabbed your coat, and headed out the door as fast as you were able. Based on my bartending training and instincts, I thought, *Something's going in that coffee besides coffee.* I suffered under this delusion for quite a number of weeks, until one night you came over and joined us.

Michael Sigman: At the time I was working overnight at a radio station. I had to get up in the middle of the day, and I would have lunch at The Sting. One day I heard your voice, and I thought, *I'm desperate for a date to go to the Milwaukee Symphony Orchestra concert in Manitowoc. I've run through everybody else I know, and they've all turned me down.* I think you ended up being number fifty-eight.

So I came over and asked you to go on a date with me the next day. The symphony was a relatively hot ticket—I wouldn't call it completely hot, but you wanted to go see it, which surprised me.

Kelly: One of the biggest risks I have ever taken in my personal life was agreeing to go out with you, because I had no idea what I was getting into. But you spoke in complete sentences, and you seemed very earnest and genuine, so I thought, *How bad can he be?* And you weren't that much bigger than me, so I figured I could take you if I had to . . .

Michael: When I picked you up for the date—

Kelly: You had a three-piece suit on. Broke my heart.

Michael: —And a red Datsun station wagon with one yellow door, which of course was further cause for concern. So we had a nice dinner, and we went to the concert—

Kelly: Where *everybody* knew you. Everybody. Every third step we took, somebody said: Hey, Michael, how ya' doing? How are your parents, Michael? It's so good to see you Isn't this a great concert? It was the first time I had ever been with anyone who was that well known within the community. You grew up in Manitowoc. Your parents had a business there; your grandparents had had a business there. You knew everybody or knew *of* everybody.

Michael: Then I brought you home to dinner.

Kelly: Your dad said, "I like this one, son. She can at least read."

Michael: My brother jumped in and said, "How good is she in bed?" But that's my brother—*Thanks a lot!*

Kelly: And then it just went from there.

Michael: We were sitting in my parents' home one day, and we had just come from your parents' house, where your mother had hollered across the house, "Hold out for a rock, dear!" So my mother brings up the fact that we had my grandmother's ring in the safe, and I just looked at you and said, "There's your rock. Happy now?" So we now say that it was my mother who made the proposal, but it was your mother who sealed the deal: Hold out for a rock!

Kelly: She knew the priorities.

Michael: So we had arranged to have first a civil ceremony, and then later on to have a religious ceremony. I left my work—"Excuse me, I have to get married"—and I walked across the street, where I met you. And Judge Hazlewood married us.

Kelly: The funniest part about everything was that everybody in town had us paired off before we paired ourselves off. Every other comment was, We thought the two of you would make a great couple! And when I'd ask them why, they'd say something like, Oh, because you're so much alike. And I thought, *Oh my God! Yikes!* But I think the best thing is just that you understand me and you support me. It's really nice to

know that, at the end of the day, I can come home to somebody who I know is in my corner.

Recorded in La Crosse, Wisconsin, on July 18, 2010.

STEVEN DAVIDSON KETCHAM, 32,

talks with his wife,

ALEXANDRA NOGUEIRA BUDNY, 29

Steven Davidson Ketcham: The first time I met your mom was when she came up to me and said, "It's a pleasure to meet you. My name is Nadia, and I'm going to be your future mother-in-law." The first words out of her mouth—I hadn't even met you! And you know what? She was right.

Alexandra Nogueira Budny: My mom had been diagnosed with breast cancer in 2001. She had just left her company, and she lost her health insurance and had to sell our house to pay for treatment. So she sold her house and rented a house your dad owned. They found out that they both had single kids in their twenties, and they decided that we were perfect for each other. My mom invited you to dinner, and the second I found out about it, I said, "Call him up and disinvite him! You're not setting me up!"

Steven: I was pretty disappointed about that, because my stepmother had showed me pictures of you, and I was, like, *Wow, she's really cute! I would love to get to know her.* I also knew that you were a writer and you were a student at Princeton. You sounded so interesting.

Alexandra: So they had to find another way for us to meet. They were sneaky.

Steven: They concocted this story: My father wanted me to help him move stuff out of his rental property. So I was taking apart my sister's playground that had been there for years upon years, and then your mother pulled up with you. And that was the first time I met you.

Alexandra: Then my mother got you to help her move too, so we spent a week together—long, long hours.

Steven: What's amazing is that there were certain moments that really could have changed everything for us. Without your brother we wouldn't be together at this moment. You had invited your ex-boyfriend to come over to help your mother move in, and I was there helping your mother as well. I remember you said, "Steve, you can go home. My mother doesn't need your help anymore, because my boyfriend's going to be here." But then your brother said, "Steve, why don't you stay? My mother would really appreciate it." If I would have gone home that day, I don't think I ever would have come back.

Alexandra: Seeing you and him together was so important—how different you were. And then my brother said, "I think you're perfect for each other, and I don't think you're going to give this guy a chance." So I had to prove him wrong. By the end of the week we were dating. Six months later we were living together in New York.

Steven: Your mother passed a couple of years later, and then my father had pancreatic cancer. I think it bonded us together, because we were forced to either support each other or just move on. And I think our parents realized that if we worked at this we could create something beautiful.

Alexandra: Today is our wedding day. We got married at around noon in city hall.

Steven: I don't even think I said I do. I said, "Of course I do! I'm the luckiest guy in the world." Because that's how I feel. I don't think I've ever been so certain about anything in my entire life, and I didn't hesitate a single moment.

Before your mother passed, I made a promise to her that I would always take care of you and love you. If you were ever in a similar situation with my father, what would you say to him before he passes?

Alexandra: I would tell him that I'm the luckiest girl in the world. I would never let you out of my grip. Ever.

Recorded in New York, New York, on July 18, 2008.

Lost

NORMA TAYLOR, 78,

talks to her daughter,

RANDI TAYLOR, 52

Norma Taylor: I was standing on the subway platform smoking a cigarette, and I turned and saw this handsome young man coming down the steps. He took my breath away. We got on the same train, and he sat across from me. I just knew that that was the man I was going to marry. I've never had that kind of feeling before, and I've never had it since. I didn't even try to flirt with him, because I knew that if I didn't meet him that day, I was going to meet him another day—he was my destiny.

We got off at the same station, and I walked in front of him. Then he said to me, "Don't you know you're not supposed to smoke on the subway?" That sort of took me off guard. I said, "No, I didn't know that." We started walking together, and he asked me what I was doing that evening. He came to pick me up later, and we went out. That's the way I met him.

Dan was kind, and he was caring, and most of all, I loved

the way he loved me. He always made me feel special, and he always encouraged me. Having grown up in a home where I felt like I couldn't do anything right, he made me feel like I had wings and I could fly. He used to go to work in the morning, and then he would call. I would say to him, "You just left," and he would say to me, "I just wanted to hear the sound of your voice."

He had been complaining that he wasn't feeling well for a long time. He went to the doctors, but they couldn't find anything wrong. So he went into the VA hospital, and they did all kinds of tests, and they discovered he had cancer of the pancreas. The doctor said that once he felt the first pain, it was already too late. We couldn't have saved him.

Shortly after he died, I started to doze off, and all of a sudden I felt a kiss on my cheek. I opened up my eyes, because I thought I was alone. There was no one there, but I could still feel his lips on my cheek.

He took wonderful care of me, and when I lost him, I was adrift. I didn't know how to take care of anything. And I had to deal not only with losing him but with adjusting to taking on the responsibility of a house and bills and children, and I had to go back to work. I really didn't know how to manage, but always, in the back of my mind, I would hear him saying, *You can do it! You can do it!* It was that love and that encouragement and that confidence that he gave me while he was alive that enabled me to carry on after he was gone. I wanted to do it for him, so that he would be proud of me.

I talk to him all the time. On our anniversary, on his birthday, and on Valentine's Day I buy cards for him and just write whatever I'm feeling. And if the tears come down and they stain the ink, that's okay. It keeps him close to me, and that's really what I need. The last card I bought was this past March first, on the anniversary of his death. I wrote, "It's 37 years, but you're still with me and you'll be with me always. You were my life."

I never wanted people to feel sorry for me that I lost Dan, because I always felt I was so lucky to have had him at all. I would've rather had him for that short time than been married a hundred years to somebody else.

Recorded in New York, New York, on March 12, 2006.

LEROY A. MORGAN, 85,

remembers his late wife,

VIVIAN

Leroy A. Morgan: When I came out of the army, they had job openings for the post office, but you had to take an entry exam. They had about five hundred guys taking this test, and I finished number eleven. Vivian was also at the post office, and I used to kid her about it. And she'd say, "Leroy, you were number eleven, but I was number two!" She never did let me forget that.

She had a beautiful smile. We used to go out for coffee breaks, and then later on we started going out to shows. About six months later I asked her, Would she marry me?

My wife and I were in Philadelphia, and we saw a sign that said SUCCESSFUL MARRIAGE. I never will forget it: It had six points to always say to your wife or husband, and the first one was YOU LOOK GREAT. The second one was CAN I HELP? The third one, LET'S EAT OUT. The fourth one was I WAS WRONG. And the fifth one was I AM SORRY. But the last and most important one was I LOVE YOU. That was it. There were six statements, and it said if you follow that, you'll have a successful marriage. So we followed it, and we did have a successful marriage.

If she was working out in the yard, I'd come out: "Can I help you?" And when we'd come home from work, and I knew she was tired, I'd ask her, "You want to go out to eat?" To keep her from working and cooking at the same time.

It lasted fifty-three years, two months, and five days. It's been rough, but every morning when I wake up she's included in my prayers, and I talk to her every night when I go to bed.

She was something. One thing: If they  ever let me in those pearly gates, I'm going to walk all over God's heaven until I find that girl. And the first thing I'm going to do is ask her if she would marry me and do it all over again.

Recorded in Chicago, Illinois, on July 27, 2007.

PATRICIA LOUISE FOREMAN-BATES, 84,

talks with her daughter

KAY LEWIS, 58

Patricia Louise Foreman-Bates: There was just something about George. I met him at a dance, and at that time he wore his hair kind of long, in sort of a ducktail, I guess they called it. I remember telling my sister Rosemary that he was such a nice guy, but I said, "I really don't like guys that wear their hair long." I got over that. He told me later that his mother said, "Do you know that she's Catholic?" Because that was an issue.

Kay Lewis: He was Lutheran.

Patricia: That's right. But that just didn't seem to matter to George. He said, "I like Catholics. They don't believe in divorce." I was twenty-three when we were married. I gave up my Irish name of Doyle to become a Foreman. I became very proud of the Foreman name. And we had seven children.

Kay: Sounds like it was love at first sight.

Patricia: It was. It really was. I loved that guy and he loved me too. Once we stopped at a restaurant, and he took you inside with him. You were probably three years old. The clerk said, "What a pretty little girl!" And he said, "You should see her mom!"

George died when he was forty. It seemed like the end of my life. I remember going to the library to look for books to help, because I thought, *I don't know how to be a widow.* It was a difficult time. In one way I made it more difficult, because I didn't want people to help me. I didn't want people to look at us and say, It's so sad about the Foreman family. I just felt like I had to work things out by myself. I wanted to keep everything as much the same as I could. I wanted you to get involved in your school activities and go to the dances.

Kay: He was always in our conversation. I think we even teased him, making jokes about the things he had done or said. You kept him very much alive for us, and you never made us feel like there was something wrong if we were laughing.

Patricia: Oh, no, no. There was joy. You know, there's a time for tears, and it isn't when you're with children who don't know the depth of your loss. I remember looking at you all and thinking, *How can they live a life without a father? This is too much to ask of them!* But I think you all rose to the occasion.

I never intended to marry again. I was a widow for twenty years, while you kids were growing up.

Kay: Never even dated.

Patricia: I remember one time a gentleman asked me out for dinner, and when I refused he said, "You know I'm not asking you to marry me. I'm just asking you to go out to dinner with me." I just didn't think about it, you know?

But one day a secretary from one of the other buildings where I work introduced me to Warren and arranged for us to go on a date. Teresa and Margie were home from college, and so they were getting me ready, doing my eyes and all this, and I thought, *What have I signed up for?* So I said, "At eleven o'clock, if I don't think that I want to be with him the rest of the evening, I'm going to call and have you come get me."

We went to a dance. Eleven o'clock I called, and I said, "He's a great dancer. Go to bed."

Kay: And you guys danced for how many years?

Patricia: Quite a few. [*Laughs.*]

After Warren's death, which was just this past February, there are times that I just feel like I need to turn and talk to him. But that's okay. You face death twice like that, and I think it's a growing experience.

I am alone, but I have never felt lonely. I'm surrounded by family. And I gave you security at one time, you are giving me such security back right now. There's been a lot of changes in my life, but it has always been love that has carried me through.

Recorded in Dayton, Ohio, on April 24, 2010.

GLORIA ROBERTS, 58,

talks about her husband,

NATHANIEL, 73

Gloria Roberts: I met Nathaniel at work. He was coming down the hall, and we just kind of exchanged hellos. It had been nine years since my first husband passed, and his wife had also passed away. From the beginning he was very down-to-earth and easy to talk to. We started growing closer and closer, and then he had asked me to be his lady. I told him no: "We're best friends. I don't need to cross that bridge." He asked me again a couple months later, and finally I told him I would give it a shot. I found it was easy being with Nathaniel, and so we were married in 1997. We had a huge wedding, and we had all of our children participate.

In 2007, Nathaniel was diagnosed with Alzheimer's disease. I think there was a part of me that said, *He's going to be just fine,* because that's how I could handle it emotionally. But I could see changes in his behavior. He could never find keys. He would go into the kitchen, and when he would come out the water would be running. Our conversations changed. He kept repeating himself, asking me the same questions over and over again. His personality had been outgoing, and now he's really quiet.

He was a ballroom dance instructor, and he's a wonderful dancer, very light on his feet. We used to do a lot of the ballroom dances: the waltz, the swing. He loved doing the East Coast Swing and the West Coast Swing and the Latin dances. He is really good at moving his hips. He doesn't remember the routines anymore—a lot of that has gone—but we still get up and dance. Sometimes I'll just put some music on and say, "Come on, we're just going to freestyle. Let's just dance." And he loves that.

He tells me daily how much he loves me, and I truly love him. Whenever we kiss it's five times: one, two, three, four, five. And everywhere we go, he lets people know: "This is my wife." When I take him to a doctor's appointment: "My wife is coming in with me—she's my everything." How can you not love that?

But sometimes I'm just sitting there, and I'll burst into tears. I miss my husband. I grieve the man he used to be. There are times when I think he's fully present. He may have a day like that, maybe two days, and then he goes back into that other place. I find myself wanting to argue, but it doesn't do any good.

When my first husband passed I was numb, and I really couldn't cry, but I find with this one I cry all the time. It's a different kind of grief, and to me it's deeper, because I can see him, but he's not there. I truly can't imagine my future without Nathaniel being in it, but I know that Alzheimer's progresses. So I've made the decision to stand and to love my husband as he is. That changes all the time, but it's all I can do.

Recorded in Seattle, Washington, on October 24, 2008.

DOLORES VELARDE, 79,

talks with her daughter

LINDA VELARDE, 54

Dolores Velarde: My mom and I went to the little Polish corner store, and I happened to see this man that looked very handsome to me. I said to my mom, "Look at him. Isn't he gorgeous?" She said, "Don't say that—you're too young!" But I looked at him, and he looked at me.

The next time I went, the owner said, "Here's a note for you. It's from this fella you were eyeing. He was eyeing you too." I went outside with the note, and he was waiting for me. He said, "What's your name?"

Linda Velarde: I think we have to note that you were just fifteen, and Dad was twenty-one at the time. So when you met him, you started talking . . .

Dolores: We would just walk the blocks. We had to be careful, because not too many Polish boys in the area looked kindly upon the Mexican people.

Linda: Eventually Dad had to go back to Mexico, because he was only here on a work program.

Dolores: When I told him that I wanted to go down there to see him, he said, "No, it's impossible." And I said, "It's never impossible. I'm gonna be there." And so I went to Mexico when I was sixteen. A cousin of mine was gonna go with me, but then she chickened out at the last minute, so I had no choice but to go alone.

I went on a train all the way down to Laredo, Texas. When I was waiting there for my bus, a squad car came by with the immigration police, and they put me in their car. They sat me down, and one officer said, "Who are you and where are you going?" I told him my name. He said, "Do you have your papers with you?" At that time you just needed a tourist card, so I showed it to him. He said, "You've got money?" I had to show him how much money I had—I had worked for a while and saved some money to take with me. And he said, "Where are you going?" So I gave him the address. And then he said, "Do your mom and dad know where you're going?" And I thought, *Oh boy, they're gonna ship me right back.* But I said, "Sure." Then he said, "What about if we called them?" I said, "Go ahead." [*Laughs.*] I thought, *Well this is the end of it.* But he let me go.

I took the bus to Tampico in Mexico, and I went to your father's address. His aunt and uncle opened the door, and I told them who I was, and they said, "He's not here, but we'll go get him." They brought him to the house, and when he saw me, he was probably saying, *Oh my God, she really did come!*

But that was it. We got married by the justice of the peace.

I just had a nice dress and a skirt—nothing traditional. His mother and his brother were there to witness our marriage.

Linda: Did you wish your mom or dad was there?

Dolores: Well, I would've liked them to be there, yes. In fact, Mom always wrote me letters and said that she missed me and wanted me back home. She said, "Dad wants you back home too, because he misses you."

I went back home with my husband, and I guess my dad forgave me. He was just glad I was home.

Linda: When you came back to the States after being in Mexico, Dad had no job waiting for him back here, and neither did you, for that matter. So you moved in with your parents. Grandma had how many bedrooms in that little apartment?

Dolores: Just two. So my younger sister and my brother had bunk beds in with my mother and father's double bed. Then we had another bed off the living room. When I got older I looked at that house, and I said, "Lord, where did we all fit?" But after my third child, we moved out.

Linda: By the age of twenty-four, you had six children from ages one to six. I am the youngest. And then you had the wisdom to stop having more. [*Laughs.*]

Did Dad ever say, "Let's stay in Mexico and raise our kids"? Or was it just understood that you would come back to Buffalo?

Dolores: No, he never objected to coming back with me. But when he got older and we traveled back and forth on vacation to Mexico, he often said, "If I die, I want to be buried here." And when he did die, we were in Mexico on a vacation, but I could not bring myself to leave him there. He had children back home, and they wanted their dad to be with them. So I brought him back again.

Recorded in Buffalo, New York, on August 10, 2008.

CINDY WHITE, 46,

talks to her friend

ERIC ERNSBERGER, 45

Cindy White: I met the true love of my life on a total fluke. I was living at my parents' and making the transition into being a single mother when I met Dan on August eleventh of 1990, at a time in my life when I said, No more men! I don't care who they are, how much money they have—I'm done with it! I've been jilted too many times. And so when I met Dan I didn't try to impress him. I didn't make up a bunch of stories, because I didn't really care much if he was interested in me or not. The fact that he was interested in me made me even more sure to give him the signal that I didn't want him. And I was just totally, brutally honest with him—that I was separated, that I had a son that was three years old, and I had a job, so I didn't need him, and on and on and on. But before too long I realized I was going to be with him forever.

About six weeks after I met Dan, my ex-husband—my son Jake's biological father—called me. I hadn't heard from him since he'd left about a year before. I was sure that he was calling just to piss me off. When I got on the phone he said, "I tested for HIV, and I'm positive." And I'm, like, "Yeah, right. You're full of crap." In the early eighties, the only thing I'd heard about HIV was that it was pretty much only happening to gay people, or if you were promiscuous or a drug dealer. So I was sure it couldn't happen to me.

And yet, when I got off the phone, I had this uneasy feeling. I was in this relationship with Dan, and I hadn't lied up until then, so I surely wasn't going to lie about this. So I called him and said, "Jake's dad called me and says that he had tested positive for HIV. What do you think?" And Dan's like, "You don't have HIV. You don't even look sick—you can't be sick." He said, "Just go get tested."

I went off to the gynecologist and got tested. And it took about fourteen working days to get your test back at that time. And about three weeks later the doctor's office called me and said, "Cindy, we botched the test. Do you think you could come down and just give us some more blood? It'll only take a few minutes, and we'll get you on your way."

The doctor took me back to an office right away, which should have been my dead giveaway that something was awry, because that never happens when you go to the ob/gyn—you always sit out front and wait a long time. Anyway, I get back there, and there's a wastepaper basket on the floor, there's a telephone, a box of Kleenex, and a glass of water on the desk. And I'll never forget that room, because after a few minutes of chitty-chatty, she said, "I just got to tell you that you're the first woman that I've ever had to say this to, and I hope the very last. Your test came back positive for HIV." I started shaking the minute she said the words to me. I burst into tears. She cried. In fact, she came over and held on to me for about five minutes because I was crying so hard.

The first thing I thought was, *Oh, my God, I'm going to die, and Jake is not going to have a mother. I'm never going to see him get out of high school. I'll never see grandchildren.* Then the next thought was, *I've got to tell Dan. I'm going to have to call my lover and say, "I love you so much, guess what? You're going to have to test for HIV, because I got it. So much for loving me, huh?"* Then the next one was my parents—my conservative, love them like I do, midwestern parents. That broke my heart, because I had spent my whole life up until that point trying to stay out of trouble so that they didn't have to be disappointed in me. And here, at a month shy of thirty, I was going to have to go home and tell my parents: I'm not going to give you another grandchild, *ever*. And guess what? I've got HIV!

Dan got diagnosed HIV positive. I said to him, "You need to get away from me. Why should you have to watch me die— how unfair is that? I mean, after all, I already gave ya HIV, so it just seems like worse torture that you should have to put up with watching me die." But Dan said, "It's a blessing that I'm HIV positive, because we can do this together."

We knew that HIV could make it impossible at some point for us to survive, but we weren't going to just give up. Dan's philosophy about life was that we only had this one to live, and that no matter what, we were going to live it to the fullest we could. Even the days we were sick—I don't ever remember those days being so fraught with illness that there wasn't something that we either smiled about or held between us that made our relationship special.

Eric Ernsberger: As his health failed, what did the two of you talk about?

Cindy: As he was dying, one of the things that he said that was so important to him was that I was well. "Boys need their moms," he said. It was almost as if he was dying for me— like if he died, then I'd live, and things would be the way he thought they should be. He was sure that Jake would always need his mom.

We brought him home in hospice care around his birthday, in October of 2001. He passed away the morning of December twenty-sixth of 2001. Dan had promised Jake and I that he wouldn't die on Christmas, because he didn't want to mess Christmas up for us.

I could not wrap my head around what it was going to be like to be alone. I mean, Dan had been in our lives for a decade. Plus, how can I be a mom and a dad to a teenager?

Jake's twenty now, and as far as he's concerned, he had a dad, and his name was Dan, and that's all there is to it. Jake is a good kid, and he learned from his dad how to be a kind, honest, trustworthy young man, and he is that.

I miss Dan every day. He threads in and out of my life in

ways that make me see why widows have always been considered a little bit daft. We don't much care anymore what people think of us. And yet, there's not a day that goes by that I'm not happy I'm alive.

The truth is, falling in love doesn't save us from the big, bad, icky things that can happen in the world. But the thing I'd want for people to know the most about Dan and I is that

we had an incredible love story despite a horrible virus. And I don't believe I'm here because of anything less than his love for me.

Recorded in Omaha, Nebraska, on June 1, 2007.

ANDREA ST. JOHN, 28,

talks to her friend

TOM "BRODY" BRODERICK, 43

Andrea St. John: At the school where I was teaching, there was this buzz of anticipation that Kevin Broderick was coming back to visit. I said, *I have to meet this guy to see what he's all about.* And when he came, he sat down at my lunch table, and I think it just started with, "Hi. How are you?" Kevin had this way of making you feel like you were the only person in the whole world. He was just there for an afternoon, but I was hooked. And then off he went, but there were rumors he was coming back to teach.

My heart skipped a beat when he walked into the faculty meeting that August. After the meeting he said, "Hey, does anybody want to go have a beer after school?" Everyone said, Yeah sure, we'll be there. And I was the only person who showed up.

Tom Broderick: Were you set up?

Andrea: Looking back on it, I think maybe. It took a while for him to build up the courage to ask me to do something alone. We had a lot of seventh grade–style dates: You know, where a lot of our mutual friends met in one place. [*Laughs.*] Then in October, we went out to dinner, and that was it.

Tom: You knew he had been in New York fighting Ewing's sarcoma before. Was that scary?

Andrea: No. I just saw Kevin. Not until he went back for the checkup scans did I really think about cancer in his life or our lives. I think at that point it was harder for Kevin than it was for me. He knew where he'd been and where he might be headed, and he was worried enough for both of us.

When he got the call from his doctors, I walked into the faculty room, and his eyes were red. I said, "Are your eyes okay?" As soon as I got the words out of my mouth I realized, *Oh no!* And he said, "I think you should get your jacket; maybe we'll go for a walk." He told me what his doctors had told him—that the cancer was back, and that it was back in a few places. I had to pull it out of him; he was trying to protect me, I think. He said, "There's a spot in my thigh, and my ribs, and in my pelvis." It was December, and he paused and said, "I lit up the scans like a Christmas tree." [*Laughs.*] I said, "Not funny!" But he just gave me that smile, and I started to laugh.

Tom: So he started treatment again, but you guys still did quite a lot, didn't you?

Andrea: We did. We never missed an opportunity to enjoy each other's company. But by the following January, he'd been admitted, and he was having radiation. It's a different ball of wax when you're an inpatient. When Kevin couldn't leave at the end of the day I think it signaled the real possibility that things could change. But we always had hope.

One night I was telling him, "I consider you my husband, and I love you so much. I just want you to know that." But he wasn't very responsive. The next morning he woke up, and I was rubbing his feet. He pointed to a photo of us that was taken in the winter, and he said, "Who do you see when you look at me? Do you see him, the guy in the picture?" He said, "Because I see the girl in the picture, the girl I fell in love with. She's the one I want to spend the rest of my life with. You are my life and my light, and I'm here now because of you."

I said, "I see the guy in the picture every time I look at you. Every time I see you, I fall in love with something new or unnew. Yesterday I fell in love again with your sense of humor. The day before that I fell in love with your freckles all over again." We both cried, and he wiped his eyes with his hollowed-out right arm, slowly. He took a deep breath and said, "Well, now that that's over with, will you marry me?"

That spring we got married with Becket, our yellow Lab. We looked around us and said, "Well, he's as good as anybody. Why not?" So he's our witness and our reverend and the keeper of what we share.

Kevin and I had this wonderful way of being in step with one another without a lot of effort. One morning I woke up and got his tea ready, and I said, "Hey, I need your opinion on something. I want to wear this dress to your wake." So I put it on, and I stood up on the bed next to his, so that he could see me. And I said, "How do I look?" He started to cry. And I said, "Oh God, I'm so sorry. I'll take it off. I didn't mean to upset you at all." And he said, "No, it's just that you look so beautiful. I'm so glad I got to see you in that dress." He kept crying, and I held his hand and sat down on the bed next to him and said, "What's going on?" And he said, "It's just that I woke up this morning more ready." I asked him what that felt like. He paused and looked at me and said, "Well, I guess it's the same thing you felt when you put the dress on this morning."

I loved him . . . [*crying*]. It was easy. From the beginning to the end, sticking by his side, it was the easiest thing I've ever done. It was an act of love. And it was effortless.

Recorded in Saranac Lake, New York, on June 20, 2008.

LISA THOMAS, 41,

talks with her mother-in-law,

ANN JAMISON, 62

Lisa Thomas: The first time that I remember seeing Mark, I was in a bar. I looked across the table, and I thought, *Wow, who is that?* Mark had a very ethereal quality. I always said he looked like a fairy or an elf of some sort, because he had these big, wide cheekbones and these eyes that slanted up.

So I went to my friend Beth, and I asked, "Who is that guy sitting at the end of the table in the fringe leather jacket?" And Beth said, "That's Mark Jamison." And I went, "Oops, never mind," because I knew he was married.

When Mark got a divorce we became really good friends. We started hanging out, and he invited me over to show me how he made neon. When I started dating him I told him, "Don't tell anybody we're dating, because you just got divorced. I don't want people thinking, *Oh, this is just a rebound relationship, and it's not going to last.*" Unbeknownst to me, he blabbed his mouth to everybody.

We didn't date very long—only a couple months—but it was an intense relationship. In a matter of weeks we began talking about children, and we were trying to get pregnant.

Ann Jamison: He told us about you. I think the words were, "Dad, you're going to love her. She has great legs." [*Laughs.*] But we hadn't met. There just wasn't the time.

Lisa: There wasn't. Everything happened so suddenly. I remember Beth calling me, "There's been an accident and Mark's hit his head." I got in the car and just drove. I walked into the hospital room, and you didn't know me, but I remember you grabbed me and said, "You made him so happy." Well, I misunderstood you. I thought you said, "You'll be so happy." And I was, like, *Okay, okay. There's hope.* And then I looked up at the chaplain, and the look on his face indicated that I did not hear you right. I said, "What? What?" And you said, "He never knew what hit him."

I had never experienced an implosion of such power. And you were so supportive. I remember thinking, *How can she be so strong?*

The funeral was horrible. I just remember being in a haze.

Ann: When we left the cemetery, I looked over to find you, and you were on the ground. Your clothes were spread out; it looked like you'd melted. It was awful. You still had the high intensity of newfound love and the future ahead. As his mother, at least I had had all the past.

Lisa: When I first went into Mark's apartment the night after he died, I looked around at the dishes we had eaten on and the wineglasses that we'd drank out of—everything was still there. And I remember not being able to leave. He loved music, and I went over to the CD player and pushed Play, because I wanted to know what he was listening to the night before. It was a David Gray album. And I sat there, just devastated.

I missed a week of my dance residency in Norfolk, Virginia, but the people down there were so kind to me. They said, "Just come when you can." I remember I took a pregnancy test the day before I left, and it came out positive. I'm like, *What am I going to do?* So I called my friend Beth, and then I called my mom and then I called my friend Linda. And they were so happy, you know? I'm, like, "How can you be happy? I can't do this by myself." And they said, You won't be alone. You won't be alone. I said, "I *am* alone."

I didn't tell anyone in Norfolk about it, but my first night I remember thinking, *I have to get prenatal vitamins, and I have to get something to drink besides coffee.* So I went to the health foods store, and I was standing in the aisle, this frail, feeble person, looking at all the billions of prenatal vitamins and all the pregnancy teas. Finally, after forty minutes of looking, I grabbed some. Right as I set them on the counter, on comes that David Gray song. I ran outside and I just cried. I was talking to Mark: "I'm going to need your help. I'm going to need everything I can get!" And I just remember feeling like he was there. I still feel him—even now, almost five years later.

Ann: You came out to tell us, and I had this stupid, big roast-beef dinner and I know you just could hardly breathe, and there was all this food, but you managed. You were eating your dinner, and you said, "Well, I have something to tell you." And it was wonderful, because you so easily could've said, *I'm just going to survive this thing within myself and my family and my close friends and be all right,* but you let us be a part of this baby. You didn't have to do that.

Lisa: That was my first time out to the house. I remember seeing your field and the mountains there, and I said, "Our kid is going to have the greatest life out here!"

And the birth itself—you were my coach.

Ann: It was a wonderful day. It was this yin-yang, best and worst, but the best kept coming up on the top, because this child is perfect.

Lisa: I tell little Mark about his father all the time. Once he said something about God, and I said, "Where does God live?" And he said, "He lives in heaven with Daddy, and he makes beautiful neon."

Ann: I love that. To me the worst thing you can do when someone dies is not talk about them, like they didn't even exist. Little Mark is our first and only grandchild, and then we got an extra daughter out of it. Sometimes I have to tell you I just love you for you, not only because you're my grandbaby's mother. This relationship truly feels like a friendship, and that's wonderful.

Lisa: It's true. I said at the beginning, "I can't do this by myself." And I didn't have to do it by myself. I couldn't do it without you— I know that. Thank you for being in my life.

Recorded in Roanoke, Virginia, on October 18, 2008.

PAUL WILSON, 93,

talks to his daughter

MARTHA "MARTY" SMITH, 61

Paul Wilson: I was working for a radio station located in the tenth floor of the Lassen Hotel here in Wichita, so I was up and down the elevator two or three times a day. One day I was waiting in the lobby for the elevator to come down, and the door slid aside, and there she stood, the prettiest girl I had ever seen. She was the operator. That first meeting there were three or four other people on the elevator, and she took all of us up, and they got off at their floors, and I was the last one—floor number ten. She opened the door, and I said, "Thank you," and she said, "You're welcome." That was the total conversation that first contact. I floated on down the hall thinking about her all that day.

On about the fifth day, I guess it was, I was the only passenger on the elevator, and she said, "Do you know where you can get some good chop suey?" How about that for an opening line? Thank goodness she broke the ice. I said, "Sure, the Pan American Café across the street." I said, "I eat there often." She said, "Oh?" She knew very well: I come down at six every evening and disappear, and I come back. I said, "I plan to eat there this evening," and she said, "Oh?" Then I realized I had an opening. I said, "What time do you get off?" She said, "Six." Now that wasn't true, but she arranged to have a bell-hop relieve her, and we went across the street at six, and we had chop suey, and we got acquainted.

I found out her name was Wilma—later she went by Louise. She found out my name was Paul. I found out that she was divorced and had a two-year-old girl. She found out I was about to be drafted; this was during the war. I couldn't help thinking, *Boy, if everything is okay when the war is over, and she's still available, I'm going to have that girl and her daughter.*

I think it was two days later, she brought that little girl downtown. Barbara was two years old. She had a little red snowsuit, a white fur hat, and a white fur muff that she was proud of. When her mother introduced me to her, she had her arms out to me, and I was done for.

I knew she was the one, I just knew it. And I know how— I'll tell you something I've never told anybody.

Marty Smith: There's something I don't know?

Paul: Yes. We had been seeing each other, going out to lunch and all of that, for about two weeks when a situation arose. Because of a storm that night, we ended up in my apartment. Nothing happened—but that's when I knew she was the one, and I think that's when she knew I was the one. That was the beginning.

Well, I did go away to war, and Louise waited for me for three years. She must have had plenty of other opportunities. I imagine she had to fend the guys off all the time. She was beautiful. She wasn't a beauty-queen type; she was a next-door type, only prettier. Never used any cosmetics, never went to a beauty shop in her life. She was just naturally beautiful. I came back from the war, rendezvoused with her at my parents' home, and we waited three days for a marriage license. We got married right there in my mother's living room.

I adopted Barbara immediately, and we had three more children. We had lots of good times together as a family, and we had some bad times. David, the fourth child, when he was about a year old we found out that he had cystic fibrosis, and it was a battle until he died at age nine. It was a long tragedy, but we survived as a family.

After the children were all gone, Louise developed Alzheimer's, and I was privileged to be her caregiver. She was brave, and she understood the situation. She still loved me. She really did. Your mother was the only woman I ever really loved. She was a wonderful woman, a good friend, a sweetheart, a wife, and a wonderful homemaker. We were real lovers, and we had a sixty-three-year honeymoon.

I still sleep in our bed. Sometimes I reach over and pull her pillow . . . [*crying*]. She was unfailingly loving. Unfailingly. Every day is a memorial for her.

Recorded in Wichita, Kansas, on October 23, 2009.

GRANVILETTE KESTENBAUM, 63,

talks to her friend

DARLENE GRIGGS, 76

Granvilette Kestenbaum: Howard and I met on Friday the thirteenth, 1969. He fell on me at a party, and I thought he was the goofiest guy I'd ever met in my life. He was a student at Columbia working on a PhD in astrophysics, but I didn't believe him. He said he was twenty-five—he didn't look twenty-five. He had a shirt that was so rumpled, and he had these old stovepipe jeans on and a pair of shoes, one of which had many, many, many rubber bands wrapped around it because the sole was coming apart. When I was going to leave the party he said, "I'll walk you home," and I thought, *What did I do to deserve this? I don't want you to walk me home!* And so he walked my friend and I home—I lived at that time in a girls' residence on West Eleventh Street in the Village—and my friend and I stayed up and talked about what a goofball he was. So some weeks later he called me, and he said, "Hello, this is Howie," and I said, "Howie who?" And he said, "Fine, thank you. Howie you?"

He later told me that he would come down after work in the lab up at Columbia and go up and down the steps, looking at the mailboxes to find my name, because he couldn't remember where I lived. But I wouldn't date him. I wouldn't. I just thought, *I can't walk around with this guy.*

So he would sit on my steps, and when I came out with a date he would say, Hi, how are you? And he would introduce himself and say, I hope you have a really good time. And my date would say, Who is that? And I'd say, Oh, he's just some guy. When I came back he'd still be sitting there. And I still wouldn't date him. At one point he got some helium balloons and he floated them up—I was on the second or third floor—and they said GRAN, PLEASE COME OUT. The girls thought that was wonderful, but I was embarrassed to death. I thought, *This guy is really crazy!*

Finally, the lady who was in charge of the residence said, "You've got to get that guy out of here!" She said, "Give him a date, for god's sake—get it over with!" So I went out and I said, "I'll date you someday." He said, "No, you'll forget me. You've got to date me now." So he said dinner. I said, "Oh, no, no, I'm not dating you for dinner." I said, "How about lunch?" He came on a Saturday for lunch, and we went to Washington Square, and he had a package of crystal mint LifeSavers and some seltzer, and he split the LifeSavers in half and he drank half of the seltzer, and then he handed me the can. But the next year, in June of 1970, we were married. And then for thirty-one years we were together.

Howard at heart was always an astrophysicist. He got his PhD, but then some years later switched to business. Howard wanted to share what was happening in the skies with me, and it was always happening in the dead of winter. We would go outside at about three in the morning in the freezing cold, waiting for some phenomena. After the third time I learned to say, "Yes, I see it! It is wonderful!" and we got to go inside much quicker, and we stayed married.

He started asking me maybe six weeks before 9/11, "Do you love me, honey?" And I said, "You will always have my deep and abiding love." I don't know why I said that. I'm glad I did.

On that day, September eleventh, I got up with Howard at five in the morning. For some reason, we had a little tiff, and when he left, he said, "I love you," but I didn't say it. He rounded that corner and I never saw him again.

Darlene Griggs: If you could say something to Howard right now, what would you say?

Granvilette: I would say to him, "How dare you take yourself out of our lives? We didn't need the money. I'd live with you in a horrible building with an elevator that didn't work and we'd have to walk up eighteen flights of steps." We were supposed to grow old together. We were looking forward to it.

I picture him with his beautiful silver hair. I see him, and I love him still. That's never going to change. And when I see him I try to just hold that picture in my mind. And he's always going to be fifty-six in my mind. I'm going to be an old, shriveled-up mess, but he will be fifty-six.

People talk about closure. There is no closure when you lose a loved one. I don't care how you lost them, your heart is always open. Edna St. Vincent Millay wrote something that affected me. It says, "Where you used to be, there is a hole in the world, which I find myself constantly walking around in the daytime, and falling into at night. I miss you like hell."

Recorded in New York, New York, on July 16, 2010.

BEVERLY ECKERT, 55,

remembers her husband,

SEAN ROONEY

Beverly Eckert: Sean had warm brown eyes and dark curly hair. He was a good hugger, one of those people that are just comfortable to be around, and a favorite wherever he went. I used to tell him I thought my family liked him more than they liked me.

He had a cerebral job, but in his spare time he liked to do really tangible things, like carpentry and plumbing, electrical, masonry—you name it. He loved to cook too. I keep rosemary in the kitchen now because the aroma reminds me of this marinade he made for grilled steak. He used our Weber grill year-round, even in the winter, even in the rain. He would be out there with an umbrella in one hand and his steak tongs in the other.

There are things I can picture so clearly still. Early evening on a summer night: We're relaxing before dinner, sitting next to each other on the stone step out back, and we each have a glass of wine. We're just watching the fireflies rise out of the lawn, steak on the grill, and we're talking and laughing.

Sean and I were together for thirty-four years. We met when we were only sixteen at a high school dance. He died at fifty. I try not to think about what I lost but what I had. For Sean and me, fate, in a way, was merciful. I know what happened to Sean, because he was able to reach me by phone from where he was trapped in the South Tower.

I was at home. I had left work when I heard about the towers getting hit. It was about 9:30 A.M. when he called. When I heard his voice on the phone, I was so happy. I said, "Sean, where are you?" thinking that he had made it out, and that he was calling me from the street somewhere. He told me he was on the 105th floor, and I knew right away that Sean was never coming home.

He was very calm. He was very focused. He told me he had been trying to find a way out and what he wanted was information. So I relayed to him what I could see on TV, what floor the flames had reached and on what side of the building. I also used my other phone, my cell phone, and called 911 and told them where Sean was and that he needed to be rescued. Sean told me that initially he was with some people that tried to escape by going down the stairs, but they had to turn back because of the smoke and the heat. They headed for the roof, but when they got there they found that the roof doors were locked.

He told me the other people were now in a conference room and that he was alone. I asked him to go back and try the roof doors again, to pound on them, and that somebody on the other side would hear him. I said, "The doors couldn't be locked. They are emergency doors." We both remembered the helicopter rescues from the roof at the '93 bombing.

Sean was gone for maybe five minutes, and then he came back to the phone. He hadn't had any success, and now the stairwell was full of smoke—he had actually passed out for a few minutes while pounding on the doors.

There was a building in flames underneath him, but Sean didn't even flinch. He stayed composed, talking to me, just talking to me the way he always did. I will always be in awe of the way he faced death. Not an ounce of fear: not when the windows around him were getting too hot to touch; not when the smoke was making it hard to breathe. He will always be a hero to me because of that.

By now we had stopped talking about escape routes. I wanted to use the precious few minutes we had left just to talk. I knew it was time to say good-bye. He told me to give his love to his family, and then we just began talking about all the happiness we shared during our lives together, how lucky we were to have each other. I told him that I wanted to be there with him and die with him, but he said no. He wanted me to live a full life. At one point, when I could tell it was getting harder for him to breathe, I asked if it hurt. He paused for a moment, and then said, "No." He loved me enough to lie.

In the end, as the smoke got thicker, he just kept whispering, "I love you," over and over. I was pressing the phone to my ear as hard as I could. I wanted to crawl through the phone lines to him to hold him one last time. Then I suddenly heard this loud explosion through the phone. It reverberated for several seconds. We held our breath; I know we both realized what was about to happen. Then I heard a sharp crack, followed by the sound of an avalanche. It was the building beginning to collapse. I heard Sean gasp once as the floor fell out from underneath him. I called his name into the phone over and over. Then I just sat there huddled on the floor of our living room just holding the phone to my heart.

I remember how I didn't want that day to end, terrible as it was. I didn't want to go to sleep, because as long as I was awake it was still a day that I shared with Sean, still a day where he had kissed me good-bye before leaving for work. I could still say, *That was just a little while ago. That was only this morning.* I knew there would never ever be another day where I could say that.

I think about that last half hour with Sean all the time. It traumatized me to the core of my being, but it was also a gift. My last memory that I have of Sean isn't about pain or fear, but it's about bravery and selflessness and, most of all, about love.

Recorded in New York, New York, on November 19, 2006.

Beverly Eckert died when Continental flight 3407 crashed near Buffalo on February 12, 2009.

Found at Last

HILDA CHACÓN, 49,

talks with her husband,

PEDRO MORÁN-PALMA, 48

Hilda Chacón: So tell me, *Calvito,* what did you think when you first met me almost twenty years ago?

Pedro Morán-Palma: I saw there was a beautiful lady sitting in this party. At first I thought that you were with somebody. Then I saw that it was my roommate who was bothering you, and I tried to rescue you.

Hilda: I was wearing a short skirt, and he insisted that I go up the stairs so he would see me from behind, and I got so mad that I was ready to beat him up. But you came to my rescue and pulled him away. I remember you apologized for him being so rude and drunk, and I just started saying, Ugh! Men! And you said, "Not all men are like that." *"Yes,* they are!"

We sat there at the top of the stairs, and we started talking like no one else was there. I told you I was visiting from Costa Rica, that I was divorced, that I had a kid that I really loved. And then I started talking about men, saying, "I don't know why people get married, you know? You marry a guy and you have to put up with so much *crap!"* How come I didn't scare you?

Pedro: You were fascinating. I was mesmerized, I think is the right word. You were the most intelligent, creative woman I'd ever seen in my life.

Hilda: It's funny, because when I met you I was totally sure that love did not exist. But there you were, with this exquisite sensibility and sensitivity. You came over with this calm attitude, very gentle, very sweet, and I felt like you could sense what I had gone through. *Still,* I thought to myself, *this man is bald!* I had always said I could never, *never* be with a bald guy. And there you were, becoming the most handsome man on earth. You have a little less hair than then, but I still think you're the most handsome man alive.

Pedro: It's hard for people to believe that we only dated for ten days.

Hilda: We cried profusely at the Phoenix airport when we said good-bye. I just thought, *This man is great, but he's here. My life is in Costa Rica: My baby is there, my friends are there, my family is there, my life is there. So it's too bad.*

A week later you called, and you said that you had gotten a ticket to Costa Rica, and that you were coming.

Pedro: My friends were saying that I was crazy. At some point I thought, *Maybe this is too much.* But suddenly I said to myself, *This is my opportunity.* Because it's something that my whole body was telling me: *You got to do this! This is the most wonderful thing that's going to happen in your life—you cannot let this go!* So that's when I decided to visit you in Costa Rica.

I always remember your eyes when you were waiting for me in the airport. The sun was shining in your eyes, and Nadia was hiding behind you. She was trying to see who the guy was.

Hilda: We went to Bahia Gigante, and the three of us sat there looking at the sea and the sunshine. You started telling me these weird things, like how grad students didn't earn much in the U.S., but they could live well. And you told me about the school system. "Hmm, that's good." I didn't know where this conversation was heading.

All of a sudden you said, "Well, I don't make much money, but if you want, we could get married, and I think the three of us could live with some dignity until I finish school." And I just thought to myself, *This man is either totally crazy or has the biggest* cojones *on earth, because after all that I said about marriage, here he is asking me to marry him?* I was shocked, and honestly, I had never thought about marrying again. But I just thought, *If I let him go I will never forgive myself, because I've never felt this connection with anyone before in my life.* And I said, "Yes."

I remember everybody being terrified, because I was marrying a guy that I had met ten days before and taking my daughter out of the country. I pretty much left everything behind to follow you.

I remember that the second day in Costa Rica, you and Nadia sat to watch a TV show. She started asking you all these questions, and little by little she started leaning on you. Then, I remember, she sat on your lap, and she put her hand over your shoulder. And I thought to myself, *This is one of the nicest images I'll ever save in my mind.* The two of you were laughing about that TV show, so happy. And that's how I picture the two of you today. You have this laughing relationship, so close and funny. Even if you stop loving me tomorrow, I could never pay you back for all the love and affection you have given my baby.

Pedro: When I met Nadia, I said, *I'm going to present myself as I am and see if she likes me.* And fortunately, things turned out well. I'm a really proud stepfather.

Hilda: People say, Everyday things kill love. I probably used to say that twenty-five years ago, before I met you. But the things that we do on a daily basis, simple things like going to get the fruit at the market or paying the bills, or just cleaning the house, they aren't chores or responsibilities but fun things when we do them together.

I told you when I met you that I don't like husbands. Boyfriends invite you to the movies or to dance and bring you flowers, but husbands just take you for granted, right?

Pedro: So says tradition.

Hilda: But you're not a traditional husband. I have this strange sensation with you—part of me feels like we met yesterday, but there's another part of me that feels like I've been with you forever.

Pedro: And it feels good to feel young with you, and at the same time to grow old with you. And it's all those things together at the same moment.

Hilda: Love you, Papito.

Pedro: *Yo también.*

Recorded in New York, New York, on April 23, 2010.

REGINA PEARLMUTTER, 81,

talks to her niece,

MURIEL SINGER, 57

Regina Pearlmutter: I didn't have a steady boyfriend until Irv came into the picture. I must have been fifteen or sixteen, because I invited him to take me to the junior prom at the high school. He was my first romance, and he asked me to marry him.

But when I was in my sophomore year in college, I went with my parents to the Catskills. We got there and there was a young man in the lobby. He said to his cousin, "Get me introduced, because that's the girl I'm going to marry."

So that night, when there was a dance, his cousin came and introduced herself to my parents and said that the young man wanted to meet me. We sat up until about four in the morning at the bar. My father came down in his pajamas looking for me, and said, "Oh, you're with him? Okay." Then he turned around and walked back up the steps. [*Laughs.*]

Muriel Singer: So they liked Morris.

Regina: My father did, but not my mother; she didn't like

him. Even though he was a young doctor, they just never got along.

Muriel: So did you have that same feeling, *This is the man that I'm going to marry?*

Regina: I thought he was wonderful that night. He was so bright and so knowledgeable. He was all of the things that I always wanted.

He swept me off my feet. We were married a few months later; I was nineteen years old. I don't think we had had more than a dozen dates, which isn't enough. I think I was too young to be married, but wartime speeded everything up.

My marriage lasted thirty and a half years. We had had our thirtieth anniversary party, and about six months later it broke up. I blossomed, I think, after that.

Muriel: So how did Irv come back into your life?

Regina: At the same time I met Morris, Irv was transferred to New York to train as a spy to be parachuted into Germany. On July Fourth weekend, I said, "I've met somebody else." It was a terrible thing to do. I was wearing his mother's ring, and I gave it back to him. I'm crying and he's crying. It was an awful evening. But that was it. The next weekend, when Morris saw that I didn't have the ring on anymore, he asked me to marry him, and I said yes. So that was that.

I was working at Macy's after school, and Irv's mother came in. On her knees this woman begged me to not give up her son. I always kept that to myself, because it was so embarrassing, and I felt so awful. I didn't know what to say. What do you say? Irv wouldn't get married for another six or seven years, but he did have a very happy marriage.

Forty-something years later my cousin Seymour called me saying he had just seen an obituary in one of the Long Island papers that Irv's wife had died. So I thought, *Oh . . .* I didn't know where he lived, but I thought that he maybe worked in New York, and I knew he was going to be an accountant. I looked in the phone book, and sure enough, the Manhattan book had his name and his New York office. So I wrote him a letter of condolence. I told him that I hoped he had a family that would be there for him, but if he wanted to cry on anybody's shoulder, mine was available. [*Laughs.*] I gave him my address and my phone number.

He said when the letter came, he recognized my handwriting. He opened it up and called me that second: "When can I see you?" I said, "Well, I don't know." I got flustered about it. Then he said he had to go and have some surgery. If it turned out all right, he would call me again. If it didn't, he wouldn't call.

So a month went by. He called and he asked if we could meet. I said, "I work, but tomorrow I get off at 3:00; I can be ready by 3:30." He said, "I'll be there at 3:31." And he was, with flowers.

I talked the entire four hours; he could hardly get a word in. I was very nervous. He said that he knew the minute he saw me that this was it. He was staying forever.

Soon after that he got sick. The cancer that they thought

they had taken out was coming back. After that, he moved into my apartment.

He lasted about four and a half years. He worked almost until the day he died—he kept right on going. And we did have a wonderful time together. He was a wonderful, wonderful companion, and he treated me beautifully. He loved my daughters, and I got very close to his family and still am.

When Irv came back into my life forty years later, what I found so wonderful was that I was able to do for him. I always felt guilty that I had given him up the way I did. But we had a good five years together. So you see me smiling.

Recorded in New York, New York, on July 21, 2005.

MURIEL SINGER *(left)*
AND REGINA PEARLMUTTER

ASHANTHI GAJAWEERA, 38,

talks with her mother,

HEMAMALA "MALA" FERNANDO, 63

Ashanthi Gajaweera: Mom, you met my father in 1965, when you were growing up in Sri Lanka.

Mala Fernando: It was my final year in school, and my aunt told me that this man was coming to see me the next day. I was a little annoyed at her, and I told her, "What is this all about?" She said, "He's a doctor, and he might even go abroad." So I told her, "*You* get married to him, and *you* can go abroad with him!" [*Laughs.*]

I was up all night, thinking, *How can I stop this?* The next morning I woke up and bathed early. Around ten o'clock in the morning I bathed again—and again at twelve o'clock and four o'clock. I stayed in wet clothes all day, thinking I would get sick. I expected to get pneumonia by evening, but nothing happened.

So now I was in my room, and I heard a car coming into our garden. My mother came and knocked on the door; I did not answer. Then my sisters-in-law knocked, but I did not answer.

Finally my father came and knocked on my door and said, "Darling, please come out. These guests have already waited for forty-five minutes. Please come out and meet them, for my behalf." I would never embarrass my father; I *adored* him. So I came out and saw this young man. He smiled at me, and I was nervous—my goodness! I could hear my heart pounding— like it's pounding now.

Finally, the moment came that they were ready to leave, and my mother comes in with a gold coin on a tray for the young man. If he liked me, he could take it. And he took it. I remember standing against the wall in the back of the living room when he took the coin. He looked at my face and smiled. For the first time, I felt something.

He was intelligent, animated, intellectual; I liked him. But I don't think it was love. I had no chance to meet any boys other than my own brothers, so this was a novelty for me.

I married him about a year and a half later.

Ashanthi: And did you ever fall in love with Daddy?

Mala: The thing is, I married your father on the day of my twenty-second birthday, and I had your sister just nine months later. I was very immature, and I was very reluctant to go abroad. But my father always told me, "Once you get married, you're a wife. You belong to him, and you have to go along with his future." I was away from home and I missed my family, but I never told your daddy how unhappy I was—I knew this was the partner my parents had chosen. This was the way it should be.

Then, when I was thirty-four, your youngest sister, Nalika, was born. It was a new beginning for us, and we were like a young couple, just married. I was more in love—and more mature.

Daddy used to treat me like another little girl before Nalika came. He would sometimes call me his daughter. After Nalika was born, I told him, "I'm not your daughter. I'm your wife. Treat me like a wife."

Ashanthi: And then Daddy died after just fourteen years of marriage.

Mala: Within that year I grew up so fast. I mean, that's the total changing moment in my life.

Ashanthi: Because you didn't even know how to write a check before that, right?

Mala: I found myself as a person for the first time. I was no more Daddy's little girl—I was a grown-up woman.

Then, when you were thirteen years old, one day you suddenly said, "Mom, you're now thirty-nine years old. It's time that you get married." So then I asked you, "How are you going to find a man for me?" [*Laughs.*] So you looked into the marriage proposals section of this newspaper we had. You circled all these marriage proposals and told me the next morning, "Mom, this is a good one."

He was a widower; I was a widow. He had two boys. So we met.

Ashanthi: It was kind of weird. [*Laughs.*] I was a teenager, and I saw you fall head over heels in love with your current husband, my stepfather.

Mala: That was the first time I really felt, *This is how you fall in love.* It was not a proposed marriage. We did it on our own, and you were the little matchmaker.

Ashanthi: I think Daddy would be very proud of you.

Mala: I think so. I have brought up my own three daughters and my second husband's two sons. I think I have accomplished a lot in my life.

Ashanthi: It'll be twenty-seven years since Daddy died, and gosh, you have changed. I mean, nobody would ever call you a little girl anymore. You're really a very independent, strong—incredibly strong—woman. You're my hero.

Recorded in Rochester, New York, on July 11, 2009.

DAVID WILSON, 66

David Wilson: I was born in Boston, Massachusetts. My parents were both domestics for white families. From a very early age, I remember my mother saying, "This is not something I want for you. Hopefully you will go to college and you will work for a corporation or work for the U.S. government, but not work for another family." I was an only child. My mother and father were pretty much there guiding me every step of the way.

I met my high school sweetheart at sixteen. We dated for two years of high school and then through college, and we decided to get married. We had three children—great, great kids. My life was very structured: I worked in management for a Fortune 500 company. Everybody came to work between 7:00 and 8:00 in the morning, and we all worked until 5:00 or 6:00 in the evening. I really never pushed the envelope in any way.

I was thirty-seven years old when I came to terms with

being a gay man. I had been in therapy for almost two years, and during one of the sessions, all of a sudden, a lightbulb went on for me: I realized that my wife was more like my best friend. So I sat down with her, and we spent pretty much an entire weekend trying to work through all the details. Later, we sat down with our three children, and I said, "Mom needs to move on with her life, and I need to move on with my own." That was a very rough patch for our family, but we all got through it.

Then I met Ron. We moved fairly quickly into an apartment and then we finally bought a house. Over a period of thirteen years, it was about as good as it gets: I had an ex-wife who remained my best friend, I had three adult children, and I had a partner.

One day in November, I came home from work and I pulled into the driveway. Ron had been raking. He was lying across a pile of leaves, and he wasn't moving. I didn't know quite what was going on. The EMTs put Ron into an emergency vehicle, and when I got to our local hospital he was dead on arrival.

My whole world kind of fell apart. Where do I go from here? I felt pretty broken at that point.

After six weeks I went back to work. I had seventeen people who reported to me, and I had to gather them together in the conference room and tell them that I had lost my partner. The questions were, Partner? I know you're divorced and you have three kids, but what do you mean "partner?" So a lot of that was about explaining, "I'm gay, but I didn't feel I could be gay at work. But here we are." I was the only senior manager in the entire organization who was openly gay. This was 1995.

I started going to meetings with other gay fathers. One meeting, in walked a man who had been fired from his job in Michigan. He stood up and told his story at the meeting. His name was Rob Compton. Then I stood up and told my story. We both continued to talk about the experiences we'd had and we decided to go out on a date. After about a year, Rob moved into the home that I had lived in with Ron. We had a commitment ceremony three years later. After that we were asked to be plaintiffs in a major lawsuit against the State of Massachusetts over the right to get married.

My kids and my ex-wife were fully supportive. My dad wasn't sure. He was eighty-five years old, and all of a sudden his only son was going to become this prominent, out, gay, black man. So I talked with Dad about some of the issues. A couple hours later, Dad said, "You're doing the right thing and you've got my support." When we got the decision from the Supreme Judicial Court, I drove to my dad's and said, "Dad, we won!" He was so excited. "Now, when are we going to have a wedding? A *legal* wedding?" Dad had been discriminated against his whole life, so for him this victory was not just for gay people. It was a victory he could be a part of, and he could not have been more proud.

We had our wedding on May 17, 2004, one of the first gay weddings in Massachusetts. I said, "Dad, I'm sending a limo to pick you up." Dad had never been in a limo; he was eighty-nine at that point. He was in the front row, and when we walked down the aisle, both his arms were in the air.

Recorded in New York, New York, on June 17, 2010.

GWENDOLYN DIAZ
talks with her husband,
HENRY FLORES

Gwendolyn Diaz: We were both professors at St. Mary's University in San Antonio, Texas. I was sitting in my office with the door open, and I noticed this man walking by . . .

Henry Flores: For me it was just a normal afternoon. I was one of the original computer nerds, when we used to work off the mainframe. I was walking down the hallway, and I noticed that the last office in the hallway's door was open. I looked inside to see who was in there, and I saw a flash of ankle, and I saw these beautiful green eyes, and I saw this blond hair, and I went, *Wow!* And then I went smack dab into the wall. I literally crashed. It was really embarrassing, so I scurried off into the computer room and closed the door. When I came out you were gone.

The very next day, at about the same time, I was walking down the hallway again, and I saw the same door open. I looked inside, saw that beautiful face, and I went, *Wow!* And I walked into the wall again, in the same, identical place. This time I went running back to my office, closed the door, and said to myself, *You idiot! You idiot! What are you doing?*

All of a sudden I heard this knock on my door. I opened the door, and it was you. You just kind of stared at me and said, "Do you have a cigarette?" We used to smoke in those days, but we've long since quit. I gave you a cigarette, and you kind of looked at me and turned around and walked away, and you didn't say a thing. I closed the door and said to myself, *Wow. She wants to talk to me. This is crazy.* So I looked around my office, and I thought, *An ashtray. If she bummed a cigarette, she needs an ashtray.* I cleaned all of the ashtrays in my office, and I tried to make myself somewhat presentable. Then I went and knocked on your door. I said, "You need an ashtray? You can have your pick—any one you want."

Gwendolyn: I remember when you came with the three ashtrays, I thought, *Hmm. Maybe there was something to that bumping into the walls.*

Henry: Why did you come and ask for a cigarette?

Gwendolyn: I was curious. The first time that you bumped into the wall, I thought, *That guy's a little uncoordinated—he should watch where he's going.* But the second time you bumped into the wall I thought you were trying to catch my attention by being silly. It wasn't until you came back with the ashtrays that I realized you'd taken notice of the new girl on the floor.

Henry: We started going out after that. The next thing I remember, we went out dancing. I wanted to kiss you, but I didn't know how to, so I asked permission.

Gwendolyn: We had been going out for a while. We weren't terribly young, and I was rather surprised when you looked at me and said, "May I kiss you?" I told you something like, You shouldn't have to ask. No one had ever asked my permission to be kissed. After you asked—I remember this—you looked me straight in the eye with a serious look, and you said, "I have to warn you. I'm very intense." I just looked at you and didn't say anything, but I was thinking, *He doesn't know what intense is, but he's about to find out!*

Henry: We've been married for a while now, and it has been an intense relationship. I was single for so many years, and I was never going to get married. But when you came into my life, I didn't even have a second thought about it.

Gwendolyn: You know, after all these years—seventeen, eighteen years—I'm never tired of being around you. I love to come home and share my day with you. It's not always per-

fect, but I wouldn't have it any other way.

Recorded in San Antonio, Texas, on February 18, 2008.

WINSLOW E. JACKSON, 61,

talks with his wife,

DOROTHY B. JACKSON, 62

Winslow E. Jackson: In 1989 on my birthday I was diagnosed with multiple sclerosis. I was married and had four daughters, and I was doing fabulous at work.

Three years later my wife left me. We divorced, and she took my daughters. That was undoubtedly the saddest time of my life. When my daughters left I really fell into a depression. I felt so stranded.

In 1996, I took long-term disability and moved to Atlanta to be at the Shepherd Center, which specializes in MS. One day I was exercising there and I noticed a lady had parked her red scooter next to my—and I want to emphasize—*my* piece of gym equipment. I looked over, and I said, "Wow. Nice red scooter!"

And she smiled and said, "Well, thank you." And I asked her what her name was. And she said, "Dorothy."

Dorothy B. Jackson: I was almost sixty, had been living with multiple sclerosis for almost thirty years, could barely walk, and didn't drive anymore. My family and closest friends were far from me and my husband of thirty-five years had died in a motorcycle accident. I was on my own. I was bewildered about where I was going or what I was going to do. I went through the motions of living, and I went to the gym to maintain my health.

I was in the gym one day and this man, who invariably used my favorite piece of gym equipment, asked me, "How do you like your scooter?" Well, I've heard lines like that before, but this time it was different.

That day we talked for fifteen or twenty minutes, and I found out that you also had MS. You played piano by ear—as do I—you played string bass for three years—as did I—you had lived in Germany and speak German—as do I. And of all things, your last name was Jackson, my maiden name. We immediately started speaking German with each other.

Winslow: We dated for a year and a half and really had a lot of fun. We were able to scrunch two scooters together in my car. Really, we could just about go anywhere. You were designated as—

Dorothy: —chief navigator.

Winslow: Until you made a mistake and took us off to Dayton when we were trying to get to Chicago, and you were demoted to junior navigator.

Dorothy: I didn't make a mistake—this is just one of your many stories. [*Laughs.*]

Winslow: But my favorite experience was probably taking

you to Chicago to meet my daughters. All of a sudden they were talking with you and not me—I was kind of left out of the conversation. And to this day it still goes on. Their favorite saying is, "Oh, poor Dorothy!"—for getting stuck with me.

Typically, it's really difficult to be a caregiver for somebody with MS. It just strains the relationship, because we look like we're healthy but inside we fatigue easily, and we have sensory problems. It's kind of an invisible disease. And a lot of relationships don't make it. So the question came up, *How can two people with MS ever survive together?* This has been the real miracle of our relationship—together we can do so much more. We've actually traveled the world.

Dorothy: There's some things that we didn't expect that make our partnership a particularly good one, such as if one of our scooters goes down, the other one has a scooter and can pull or push the other one.

Winslow: I've pulled you many times.

Dorothy: And I've pulled you.

Winslow: Today they have medications that can almost stop the progression of MS. So my symptoms, believe it or not, have not really changed in the last ten years. And your progression is the same. So I certainly am very hopeful that MS doesn't worsen or stricken me to the point that I'm bedridden. I'm very hopeful that you will not worsen either, so we can continue to enjoy life to its fullest.

Dorothy: We'd like to think that we're setting good examples of how to live life and have fun.

Winslow: Every day is exciting. Dorothy, thank you so much for being with me.

Dorothy: You're so much fun to be with. Every day I awake and wonder what surprise you have in store for me. I look

forward to continuing to see the world with you.

Recorded in Atlanta, Georgia, on August 12, 2010.

GLEN PARDY, 55,

talks with his wife,

SUE STEINACHER, 54

Glen Pardy: You came into my store. I owned a sign business in Fairbanks, and you worked for a government agency that needed a sign produced. And what ordinarily would have been a five- or ten-minute business meeting turned into a two-hour discussion of virtually everything under the sun.

Sue Steinacher: I still remember what you were wearing: that black shirt with the Nehru collar. What was a good thing, though, was that you were behind the counter, so I didn't actually see that you wore black Velcro sneakers with white socks. But from the waist up you looked pretty good.

Glen: You looked pretty good head to toe, and I thought, *Who is this tall, slender beauty?* But I had always maintained something of a business philosophy that one shouldn't necessarily hit on a customer. So we did the business transaction, and we manufactured a sign that said WELCOME TO ALASKA, and it's still at one of the border crossings into the Yukon. But once the job was done you left town. Four years passed by until you needed another sign.

Sue: We went through the whole process of designing and building and getting it installed—and you still hadn't made a move. Finally, I called you up and said I was ready to go out to dinner with you.

Glen: So we did. You were in town for seven days, and we went out five of those seven evenings. You went back to Nome, and we alternated phone calls and faxes. This was before either of us were e-mail people. We argued by fax. We told jokes. We made lists. We stayed in pretty serious touch.

Sue: I found that our first year of a long-distance relationship was actually a really good thing. You've got great handwriting.

Glen: You seemed actually interested in searching my soul to find the real person within. That was a new dynamic for me.

Sue: As hardheaded and as independent as I seemed, I had sunk to the point in some relationships where I thought, *This one will really give me the love I want if I could only bake the perfect strawberry rhubarb pie or if I could only climb mountains faster*—all these crazy ideas.

But I had come to a point where I wasn't going to compromise anymore. Someone either had to choose me wholeheartedly or I would make the choice to just continue living alone.

Glen: It was an easy choice. I knew I'd found not only a lovely and attractive woman but in some ways the girl of my dreams. You had done so many interesting things: traveling to

Russia; living in a log cabin without running water; raising a dog team; explorations by dogsled, and any of a number of other pretty amazing things for a gal from Long Island.

Sue: I'd always been chasing after men who I thought were what *I* wanted to be, or a more dynamic version of myself, and I would sort of graft off of their dynamism. And you were the opposite of that, because you fall into the "steady" category. I once called you a Boy Scout.

Glen: Which I thought was a compliment.

Sue: I know, and I didn't. I just thought, *Oh, he's just too nice, he's too steady, he's too reliable.* But I really felt like there was something here I had to hang on to.

We moved in together after a year. It was a big move and a bold move. But you know, at our age it was time to be bold. And we got along so well right off the start, didn't we?

Glen: It's true. I spent twenty-five years building and maintaining and struggling with a business and being so set in my ways that I could not imagine doing anything else for a living. Toward the end of that twenty-five years I was burned out and trying to think of a way out. Then you came into my life. Two weeks after we were married you got a job that paid pretty well, and I threw out everything I'd done for my adult life and went off to Nome with my new bride, not knowing what I was getting into. You can still grow, you can still change, and you've taught me all that.

Sue: We learned it together. And it was that business of yours that brought us together in the first place.

Glen: No, it was the yellow pages, dear.

Sue: That's right. I caught you telling somebody that I had asked all around Fairbanks, "Who built those big beautiful sandblasted wooden signs?" And that's how I had found you. I had to correct you by explaining, "No, I was looking in the yel-

low pages, and your shop was the closest to my office." But it was the right choice. You're my complement. You gave my life an anchor, and I'd like to think I've given your life wings.

Recorded in Nome, Alaska,
on February 14, 2009.

THOMAS PETER HEADEN, 66,

talks with his wife,

JAQUELINE MARIE HEADEN, 65

Thomas Peter Headen: I was at a skating rink one night when I was sixteen, in 1958, and I saw this young lady skating around. I waited for her to take a break and get a Coke before I made my move. I grabbed you by the hand and said, "My name's Thomas Peter Headen." And you said, "My name's Jacqueline LeFever." I looked in those big green eyes, and it was a done deal.

So we dated. Then, in 1959, your father got transferred to Japan. I decided, *Well, I'll go get her.* So I joined the Marine Corps, and I said, "I want to go to Japan." The Marine Corps said, "You'll go to Japan when we tell you you can go to Japan." So I went to a base in California.

Jaqueline Marie Headen: I dated a marine while I was in Japan, and I ended up getting married—I guess just because I thought that's what I was supposed to do. We came back to the States in 1962, but I didn't know what happened to you. What were you doing then?

Peter: Well, I finally got orders to Okinawa. And I said, *Oh, boy. I'll go see Jackie when I get to Japan!* I was home on leave—you always get leave before you go overseas—and stopped by to see your mother and say hi. And she said right away, "Jackie got married. But here, you can have this picture of her." I made some excuse that I had an appointment or something—the walls were kind of crawling in on me—and I left.

I went overseas to Okinawa for fourteen months, and then I came back to Camp Lejeune, North Carolina, not knowing that you were right outside the gate of that base.

I got discharged, and I went home to Maryland. One night the phone rang—it was you.

Jackie: I came to visit my mom. And I was calling your mother to see where you were, and you answered the phone—I was shocked, needless to say.

Peter: You picked me up, and you said, "I want to show you something." We went to your mother's house, and here was this little baby sitting there. Your daughter was about three months old, and she had those same big green eyes.

You went back to North Carolina, and I reenlisted in the Marine Corps for another six years. That was 1964, and I said, "Send me overseas." I didn't want to be down in North Carolina where you're sitting outside the gate. So I left on the twelfth of August for Vietnam. I came back to the States after twenty-six months and was stationed at Camp Pendleton, California.

One day I was sitting in the barracks and thinking about

you, and I said, *I'm going to write her a letter.* So I wrote you a letter and told you how I felt, because we were going back to Vietnam and I didn't want to be thinking about you on another tour in Vietnam. So I sent a letter off, and I was in Vietnam for four months before I even got an answer. And the first sergeant gives me the letter. He says, "You never get any mail, Headen." It was a letter from you.

Jackie: I don't know how the letter that you wrote found me. It was forwarded four times before I got it. You said, "I just have to get this off my chest—I love you. I've always loved you. I just have to say it and get it over with, and I'm done." In the meantime I had had another child—a little boy. So there I was in an apartment with two little babies and just miserable, actually. I got married for all the wrong reasons. But I came from a divorced family, and I didn't want my kids to have a broken home.

Peter: When I came back from Vietnam I spent twenty-four hours at home, and then I went to my mother at about four in the morning and said, "I've got to go to North Carolina." And she kind of looked at me: "I think you better leave that one alone—she's married. But I guess you got to do what you got to do." I said, "Yeah, I got to do what I got to do."

Jackie: I sent you away.

Peter: That was September twenty-fifth, 1968.

Jackie: Thirty years after that, I left my husband. It wasn't easy. My kids were grown, they had their college education, they had their families, but I was lonesome and miserable.

Peter: I was sitting there one night, and the phone rang—matter of fact, it was September the twenty-fifth, 1998.

Jackie: That night—I had just made up my mind: *I am out of here. I'm so unhappy.* And I sat there—and I said, *Nobody ever loved me but Peter.* And that's when I thought, *I'm going to go find him.* And so that's what I did.

I asked the operator, "Do you have a T. P. Headen in Waldorf?" And she said, "No." And I said, "Well, I'm really desperate to find this person. I know he's in Charles County, Maryland, somewhere." And she said, "Let me check." She said, "I have a T. P. Headen in White Plains."

So I said, "Oh, my God, that's it! That's him!" I started crying, and I said, "I have been trying to find this person for thirty years, it's the love of my life." And she said, "You want me to dial the number for you?" I said, "Yeah, you can dial the number." She said, "Can I stay on the line?" I said, "I don't care what you do!"

Peter: And you said, "You know who this is?"

I said, "Yeah, I know exactly who this is."

You said, "I bet you're mad at me."

I said, "No. Matter of fact, I'm still in love with you."

Jackie: I felt like I was fifteen all over again. We just talked like it never had been all those years in between. We decided we would meet in Memphis, and I picked you up at the airport. You jumped in the car and gave me a big old kiss.

Peter: We got married in May, the fifteenth. I took you down to Key West and out on a three-masted schooner, and we married at sunset. There's no address on our marriage certificate, just a longitude and a latitude.

It's worked out well. It's just sad, the time we lost—you can't get that back. We could have been together when we were eighteen, nineteen, you know? But I got you back. And you're just as beautiful as you were when you were fifteen.

Jackie: That's because you make me feel beautiful.

Recorded in Charlotte Hall, Maryland, on June 4, 2009.

JO ANN CHEW, 82,

talks with her husband,

ROBERT CHEW, 70

Jo Ann Chew: My father said if he sent me to college, I could choose one of two things: I could choose a secretarial course or I could choose home ec, because, he said, "I know you'll be somebody's wife." So I decided home ec was the way to go.

Robert Chew: Are you still cooking today?

Jo Ann: Not today. I have been up to this point, but I have Alzheimer's. My doctor told me he doesn't want me to cook— and that was music to my ears!

Robert: So how did we meet?

Jo Ann: You came to our church and I'm trying to think . . . Somehow we got together, and I don't even remember how it was. I bet you remember.

Robert: Remember the Christmas parties?

Jo Ann: Oh, yeah—that's right. I called you up and I said, "What are you doing over the holidays? I've got a lot of invitations to parties and I don't have anybody to escort me." After a few months my heart began to beat a little faster, and I think yours did too. Then we decided we wanted to spend the rest of our lives together, and we got married.

Robert: So had you thought about remarrying?

Jo Ann: No. No, no, no, no. It wasn't in my book. I just thought I was too old to be thinking of that. And I kept trying to dissuade you from marrying me, because I was ten years older than you were, and I knew that there would come a time when I would be a little old lady and you would still have all the marks of a ten-year-younger man. How old was I when we got married?

Robert: Seventy. That's not old. That's how old I am.

Jo Ann: Yeah, but you weren't then. But here we are, still together.

Robert: And you're still ten years older. Does that bother you today?

Jo Ann: It bothers me that I'm as I am. I don't want to be a burden . . .

Robert: The diagnosis of Alzheimer's—

Jo Ann: —is not pretty. I had hoped that I'd just fade off and you wouldn't have to take care of me. I'm sad, just not having control of my thoughts and my actions, and knowing what's going to be. I don't think it's fair to you. We still go to dances, and we can do things, but I don't want to be an ugly lady that's lost her head.

Robert: You'll never be an ugly lady, sweetheart.

Jo Ann: But you could have some cute little chick that you could be running around with ten years younger.

Robert: I have my princess right now.

Jo Ann: Oh, you're wonderful.

Robert: You know I still love you, more than ever. I tell you that every night. I think the feelings that I have are pretty close to the feelings that I had when we first met—probably stronger. It is my wish to care for you. Eleven years ago I said

 that, and I'm still saying that: It is my wish to care for you. But more than that, my life is yours.

Recorded in Little Rock, Arkansas, on October 17, 2006.

LISA ANN COMBEST, 46,

talks to

JAMES HANSON-BROWN, 47

Lisa Ann Combest: We got married January 11, 1986, the year I graduated from college. I remember the minister who married us was, like, "You guys are the best-matched couple I've ever talked to! You're going to be married forever." And I was, like, *Of course we are!* You know? But I guess we were in our marriage for about a year when I started thinking that something was wrong. It was all our friends could do to keep their hands off of each other, and I wanted to be physical with you, but you were kind of, like, No, not today. I have a headache.

So when did you start to realize that our relationship really wasn't what you needed?

James Hanson-Brown: Probably about three or four years in. I realized that I was gay just a little bit after my parents passed away. My mother had somewhat suspected I was gay, and she wasn't supportive. Her idea was basically that gays should be rounded up and put on their own little island and left to die.

Lisa: East Texas; that's not the most wonderful place to come out.

James: Yeah, it's definitely not the San Francisco of the South. I guess it all just built up to one night, when I kind of had this realization: *Oh my God, I'm gay.* And part of me was, like, *No, this can't be, because I love Lisa, so evidently I'm wrong.* But of course I knew I wasn't.

Up until that point I had been lying to myself, and from that point on I was lying to the one person that I would never lie to. That got to be a little too much. So for that year I was probably the worst person to live with.

Lisa: The weekend that you came out, you sat with me on the couch, and you're, like, "I have to talk to you." I remember I said, "Oh good," because I knew something was going on, and I'd been begging you to tell me what was wrong. And when you told me, I thought to myself, *Oh is that all?* [*Laughs.*] At that point it was a relief to me, because I had been thinking that there was something wrong with me the whole time, and I was wondering what I'd done.

Then you said that you were going to go away for the weekend and let me think. You came back home, and I remember telling you I didn't care if you were gay—I loved you. I wanted to stay in the relationship with you, but you were pretty adamant about not doing that.

I think it was six years before I dated anyone else, and then

I went through my dating-everybody-in-Houston phase. I guess the same thing that people in their early twenties go through, I went through it in my early thirties—the wildness, the staying out all night and everything.

Do you remember what you said to me right after I had met Todd? You said you wished that I would allow myself to be loved like I deserved. And so Todd owes you a debt of thanks, because that was when I let myself realize that he was the guy that I wanted to marry.

I think I'm a better person from everything that I've gone through with our breakup. I know the depths that I can go to and still come out, and I think that's a really great gift. So one of the things that I want to say to you is: Thank you for having the courage to be honest with yourself and with me, and for giving us the life that we deserve.

James: We've never really untangled our lives. We've always been there for each other, through everything. We are best friends, and if people don't get it, I feel sorry for them. You have to have someone like that in your life to understand it, someone that you can completely count on in any situation and that you completely love and know that they completely love you. Just in this case, it doesn't happen to be my wife. It happens to be my best friend.

*Recorded in Houston, Texas,
on December 11, 2009.*

RON MILLER, 61,

talks with his wife,

PEPPER MILLER, 57

Ron Miller: Pepper would describe me as a ladies' man, and I was. Twenty-five years ago, I knew a lot of women, I dated a lot of women, and most of the relationships were fairly shallow. But my conversations with *you* weren't shallow.

Pepper Miller: I can't pinpoint when I fell in love with you, but I remember one time you left a message on the answering machine: "Hi, this is Ron. Just checking on you, baby." I absolutely loved that. I remember saving that message on the machine, and I would play it and play it. That did it for me. But when you first broached the subject of marriage, I was, like, "I can't marry you."

Ron: But I didn't quit.

Pepper: No you didn't, thank God. We had a big wedding, and it was exciting. Walking down the aisle as Pepper Hunter and coming back down the aisle as Pepper Miller, that was a little startling. But I got into it; I enjoyed being Pepper Miller. We had a good life.

But things changed, and I began to feel like our marriage was all about you, and I wanted it to be about me too. So we got divorced. It was painful. We went to the same church, and you moved to the other side of the church. I felt like giving you the finger several times, but then I moved on. You dated people, and I dated people.

Ron: I poured myself into my work. But it was hard; I missed you.

Pepper: I missed you too. I did. Remember when you called me and you had the flu? I came and made you some soup. After tucking you in, I remember smelling your cologne on me. I missed the smell of your cologne. It's those little things that you miss.

I would call my girlfriend and say, So and so is a really nice guy, and I have a good time with him, but . . . And my girlfriend said, "Well, the problem with this guy is he's not Ron, and the problem with the other guy is he's not Ron. . . ." I didn't want to believe that. We were divorced: You had moved on, and I had moved on. Then my girlfriend said, "Don't hold Ron hostage to the past." When she said that I started crying, and she's like, "If you don't care about him, why are you crying?" Those words freed me to look at the possibility of us getting back together. I was, like, *I've got to call him.* So I called you, and we started talking. And you were just a sweetheart. We started dating, and it was good.

Then I took my dad on a cruise. We were unpacking on the ship, and in my suitcase there was this long letter from you, asking me to marry you. It was just a pouring out of your heart. That was in August. In December, we were married.

Ron: We were married eight years the first time, we were divorced five years, and this December it will be ten years we've been married again.

Pepper: We still have our bumps, huh?

Ron: Yeah. I guess we've learned that we're always going to have our bumps, but there's nobody that we'd rather be with than each other. The lesson is to hang tough and to do the necessary things to make it work.

Pepper: And to continually be grateful. We have been through a lot together, but I'm still excited to be with you. And

I'm always grateful when I can snuggle with you and smell that cologne.

Recorded in Chicago, Illinois, on February 24, 2011.

MARTHA WARD, 68,

talks with her husband,

FRANK ASERON, 65

Martha Ward: In the middle seventies you and I were both in New Orleans, on our bikes with our kids strapped on the back, and we'd see each other around. I remember you had this incredible smile that lit up the world.

Frank Aseron: Thirty years later, I saw you again at the green market.

Martha: I had just gone to a voodoo priestess the day before for a reading, and she had told me that I was going to meet a sensitive, intelligent person, and I told her, "No way!" I'd been married. I was happily divorced, and I loved my life as it was—I was single forever—so I sort of laughed at her. But there you were, and you still had that incredible smile. You invited me to the ballet, and so I said, "Okay, let's go out."

The first date was wonderful. But I told my daughter, "I don't know what the rules are anymore." And my daughter said, "Oh, Mom, there aren't any rules anymore! Just enjoy yourself!" But the most important date for us was actually New Year's Eve. At the end of the evening you asked me if I would kiss you.

Frank: You said yes. And it was such a sweet kiss.

Martha: And that was the night that we both decided: This is something special.

Eight months later, August of 2005, was Katrina. I told you that my house was an ark, and I didn't intend to leave.

Frank: I remember I was at my house really early Sunday morning, boarding it up, and I happened to turn on the TV and saw that the hurricane was as big as the Gulf. I said to myself, *What's more important: finish boarding up my house and hope that the hurricane is not a Category 5, or just leave everything and get us out?*

Martha: You tricked me into leaving. You called my daughter in Houston, and you told her, "You're the only person who your mother will listen to." So she called me early that morning and said, "I want you to get out!" Just then you walked in, and you said, "Let's leave." I didn't even make the bed. I just crammed some things in a suitcase, and I said, "Okay, we'll leave."

You were so calm. You knew what to do. You took care of me, and you weren't going to abandon me. I trusted you with my life.

By Monday night it became obvious that the city had flooded and terrible things were happening. Then, Tuesday night we saw flooding in your neighborhood, and you realized that your house had water in it. Your response was so sweet and so genuine and loving. You said, "This hurts, but it's just a house. The important things are not hurt; they are not wet."

And I thought, *I'm going to marry him.* So I put my arms around you, and I said, "We can live in my house; I know it's safe. We'll make it work, no matter what."

We moved back to New Orleans together six weeks later. We moved into my house that I determined never to share with another man. And then, in February, you asked me to marry you.

Frank: I asked your daughter's permission to propose to you, and she said, "My fear is that my mother's going to tell you no."

Martha: Well, I had certainly told all the other men who asked me no. But I had secretly already decided to say yes, and you must have known that.

You made reservations at Martinique restaurant with all of our family. And you got down on your knees and said, "Just think about it." But I'd already thought about it. I had seen you when the chips were down. When there's a terrible tragedy, you know what kind of person someone is. And so I said yes. It was the best decision I ever made. And I think we'd have blown it if Katrina hadn't happened. I think you would have stayed a bachelor, and I would have stayed a spinster, and we would have stayed in our separate houses, and we wouldn't have ever dared and braved and cleaned out enough stuff to make it work. [*Laughs.*]

I could never have imagined anything as traumatic as Katrina, and I would never have imagined anything as wonderful and incredible as meeting you and finding you and keeping you.

Recorded in New Orleans, Louisiana, on April 11, 2010.

LAUREN WEITZMAN, 50,

talks with her husband,

STUART DRESCHER, 61

Lauren Weitzman: I was thirty-five years old and living in Richmond, Virginia. There wasn't anyone significant in my life, and somehow a lifelong partner didn't seem to be in the cards for me; I was coming to peace with that. Then I bumped into an old friend at a conference. I started talking with him, but somebody else was standing there.

Stuart Drescher: I don't think that you looked at me once during the whole conversation, but I was fascinated by you. And when you walked away, I said, "I have to meet her."

Our friend said, "She usually goes to the social hours at the end of the afternoon presentations," which I never participated in, but I showed up. And there I was, talking to you for the first time. There was this fascination with you that was almost magnetic. It felt like we'd known each other for a very, very long time.

Lauren: I was a bit dismayed to realize that you were living in Salt Lake City. There was the excitement of just feeling really close and connected, but then we had to go our separate ways. And so we began this long-distance thing: I was in Richmond, Virginia, you were in Salt Lake City, and our airline carrier was Delta. So we'd either fly through Cincinnati or we'd fly through Atlanta. Somebody—I think it was me, you think it was you—decided that since we're traveling through these airports, Wouldn't it be fun to leave notes for each other that the person could find on their next way across?

Stuart: We'd write a bit of poetry or some form of appreciation, or just a thought. Then we would fold them up and tuck them under a chair in the loading areas and send a map to the other person with the concourse and the gate area, and X marks the spot.

Lauren: Although we'd only known each other for a few months at this point, it didn't seem right to spend Thanksgiving apart. It was a wonderful holiday, and when I flew home I knew I wanted to leave you something. So as I was heading from Salt Lake to Cincinnati, the only thing I could think to put on the note was "Will you marry me?"

I wasn't ready to tell you about the note, but I was definitely ready to write it. It was probably the longest I ever sat with a decision. [*Laughs.*] But you're a patient man, and in March I finally gave you a map to find the note.

Stuart: I flew to Cincinnati, and my plane was delayed in landing. I found myself running down the concourse, hoping to get to the next plane in time. I was running at a pretty good clip, and all of a sudden I remembered the note. I was debating, *Should I stop and risk my connection?* But I had to see if I could grab that note. So I peeled into the gate area and identified which chair it was. There was a fellow sitting there, wearing a very expensive suit, and I walked over and said, "Excuse me, I think I dropped my pen when I was sitting here previously," and I reached under the seat. I grabbed the note, took off running down the hallway, and got to the gate just before the door swung shut.

Lauren: Back in Richmond, I was thinking: *Would you find the note? What were you going to think when you got it?* I ducked out of a faculty meeting early and drove out to the Richmond airport. I had a big bunch of flowers, and I felt just like a bride waiting for her groom.

I still remember you walking off the plane, and the minute I saw you I knew you had found the note. You just had that glow. I had the bouquet of flowers, and we gave each other a big hug, and you said, "Yes!"

Recorded in Salt Lake City, Utah, on April 19, 2009.

ACKNOWLEDGMENTS

Special thanks to Lizzie Jacobs, who pulled this book together with skill and grace. Her deft editorial eye and singular management skills helped shape every page of this book. Lizzie was ably assisted in her work by Isaac Kestenbaum and Nina Porzucki, with significant contributions from Kate Parvenski, Ebonie Ledbedder, Melina Moore, and Maya Millett. Gratitude to fact-checkers Beth Schwartzapfel and Darren Reidy, as well as to the Audio Transcription Center and Jennifer Kotter. Thanks also to Kathrina Proscia, an early reader of this book.

We feel so fortunate to be published by Ann Godoff and represented by David Black. At the Penguin Press, sincere thanks also to Scott Moyers, Tracy Locke, Lindsay Whalen, and Liz Calamari.

Most of all, profound thanks to the entire StoryCorps family—supporters, staff, interns, volunteers, partners, and participants. You give this work life.

STORYCORPS IN BRIEF

StoryCorps' mission is to provide Americans of all backgrounds and beliefs with the opportunity to record, share, and preserve the stories of our lives. With a relentless focus on recording the stories of people who are often excluded from the historical record, StoryCorps captures lives that would otherwise be lost to history and reminds the nation that every story matters and every voice counts.

Over the past eight years we've given 75,000 Americans the chance to record interviews about their lives, pass wisdom from one generation to the next, and leave a legacy for future generations through our archive at the Library of Congress. We also share edited excerpts of some interviews through weekly NPR broadcasts, animated shorts on *POV*, our website, podcasts, and books. We hope these stories illuminate our shared humanity and how much more we share in common than divides us.

StoryCorps stories are recorded in three types of venues:

- our stationary StoryBooths, located in select cities across the nation;
- our MobileBooths, specially equipped AirStream trailers that travel the country and make extended stops in cities and towns from coast to coast each year;
- our Door-to-Door service, where StoryCorps' facilitators use portable equipment to record interviews with participants at the location of their choice.

StoryCorps partners with more than five hundred community organizations nationwide each year to ensure that we capture the widest diversity of stories possible. To this end we have also launched a series of successful special initiatives including:

- the September 11th Initiative, helping families memorialize the stories of lives lost on September 11, 2001;
- StoryCorps Commemorate, preserving the stories of people with Alzheimer's disease and other forms of memory loss;
- the Griot Initiative, the largest collection of African American voices ever gathered;
- the Historias Initiative, Latino and Hispanic American stories collected across the nation;

- StoryCorps Legacy, preserving the stories of people with life-threatening conditions;
- the National Teachers Initiative, honoring the work of educators and their impact on our lives.

We're working to build StoryCorps into an enduring national institution that celebrates the dignity, power, and grace that can be heard in the stories we find all around us. In the coming years we hope StoryCorps will touch the lives of every American family.

Lead funding for StoryCorps comes from the Corporation for Public Broadcasting.

Corporation
for Public
Broadcasting

Major funders include: the Atlantic Philanthropies, the Ford Foundation, the Marc Haas Foundation, the Kaplen Foundation, the Lower Manhattan Development Corporation, the John D. and Catherine T. MacArthur Foundation, and Joe and Carol Reich.

Additional funders include: the BayTree Fund, the Lucius N. Littauer Foundation, the National Endowment for the Arts, and the New York City Department of Cultural Affairs.

Legal services are generously donated by Latham & Watkins and Holland & Knight.

For a complete and current list of all of our supporters, please visit our website: www.storycorps.org.

National partners include:

ABOUT THE AUTHOR

Dave Isay is the founder of StoryCorps and the recipient of numerous broadcasting honors, including five Peabody Awards and a MacArthur "Genius" Fellowship. He is the author/editor of numerous books that grew out of his public radio documentary work, including two storyCorps books: *Listening Is an Act of Love* (2007) and *Mom: A Celebration of Mothers from StoryCorps* (2010)—both *New York Times* bestsellers.